M

A Pilgrim's Digress

a pilgrim's digress

MY PERILOUS, FUMBLING QUEST FOR THE CELESTIAL CITY

John D. Spalding

Harmony Books / New York

Published by Harmony Books, New York, New York.
Member of the Crown Publishing Group, a division of Random House, Inc.
www.randomhouse.com

HARMONY BOOKS is a registered trademark and the Harmony Books colophon is a
trademark of Random House, Inc.

Printed in the United States of America

Design by Leonard Henderson

Library of Congress Cataloging-in-Publication Data
Spalding, John D.
A pilgrim's digress : my perilous, fumbling quest for the celestial city /
John D. Spalding.
1. Religion.   I. Title.
BL50 .S627   2003
291.4—dc21   2002009429

ISBN 1-4000-4653-X

10 9 8 7 6 5 4 3 2 1

First Edition

For Debbie

Acknowledgments

On his journey to the Celestial City, Christian, the determined wayfarer in John Bunyan's *The Pilgrim's Progress*, encountered kindly folk, fellow pilgrims who offered him support, companionship, and sound advice along the way. This book owes its existence to several such pilgrims. Many thanks to:

Jake Morrissey, my wise, gracious, and ever-supportive editor at Harmony Books, and his bosses, Shaye Areheart and Linda Loewenthal, who read the manuscript, believed in its merit, and showed me the money.

Tom Grady, my agent, for encouraging my work over the years and finding the perfect home for this book.

The staff at Beliefnet.com, where many of these stories first ran. I'm particularly grateful to my editor, Paul O'Donnell, a brilliant wordsmith and all-around mensch, and top dogs Steve Waldman and Elizabeth Sams. They not only indulge my various whims, they showcase them.

David Heim and Don Ottenhoff at *The Christian Century*, and Paul Baumann and Margaret Steinfels at *Commonweal*.

They published some of my early adventures in religion, several of which appear in this volume.

Joshua Odell, Jeff Castello, Steve Healey, Mark Taylor, Dan Denton, Robert Plunket, James Wilcox, Trish Reynales, Mary Beth Crain, Dan Wakefield, Phyllis Tickle, Lynn Garrett, Henry Carrigan—friends, writers, or editors who have, wittingly or unwittingly, inspired or helped me.

My family members—especially my wife, Debbie—whose love, support, and good humor sustain me.

The Commonwealth of Pennsylvania, which somehow managed to be the setting for no fewer than five stories: "God's Smackdown," "A Tree Stand Close to Heaven," "All the Luck in the World," "Hallowed Be Thy . . . Whatsyourname," and "Fear and Trepanation." Whether or not this is just a coincidence, the Keystone State has certainly been good to me.

And finally, all the people featured in this book, for allowing me into their lives and for sharing their stories with me.

Contents

The only maps and charts he had to go by were remembered or imaginary but these were clear enough.

—JOHN CHEEVER, "THE SWIMMER"

A Pilgrim's Digress

Preface

Years ago I stumbled across a copy of *The Pilgrim's Progress,*
John Bunyan's classic tale about a guy who trekked across
strange lands in search of the Celestial City. I was on break
from divinity school, and I was browsing through a bookstore
in Cambridge, Massachusetts, looking for a light, entertain-
ing read after a semester spent wrestling Kant. Flipping
through the book, I recalled a Sunday school lesson in which
the teacher, Miss Stanton, a bony spinster whose heavy perfume and vivid depictions of eternal damnation still haunt
me, urged us to see ourselves as Bunyan's main character—
a miserable pilgrim named Christian, who lugs his sins
around in a backpack, gets attacked by hideous demons, and
is almost swallowed by the River of Death before he reaches
heaven's gate. Bunyan's story is an allegory of the life of
faith, and Miss Stanton's point was that if we kids didn't do
some serious business with Jesus, things might not turn out
as well for us as they did for old Christian.

I slid Bunyan back on the shelf and grabbed P. J. O'Rourke's *Holidays in Hell* instead. But on my way to the register, I doubled back for *Pilgrim's Progress*. As a div school student, I reasoned, I should probably have more than just a terrified Sunday school student's knowledge about what is widely considered one of the great works of religious imagination. Little did I know I'd one day want to plunder Bunyan's allegory for a book of my own.

What I found in *Pilgrim's Progress* surprised me. Aside from its stern Puritan message, it's a satire that is still fun to read three hundred years after it was written. On his journey, Christian negotiates his way through a world full of hypocrisy, corruption, and self-deceit. Consider the names of people he meets: Mr. Implacable, Mrs. Inconsiderate, Lord Hate-Good, Feeble-Mind, Mr. Money-Love. There's Ignorance, a fool who does not suffer wise folks gladly, and Talkative, who is "more comely at a distance than at hand." Whether you are a fundamentalist or an atheist, a Buddhist or a Muslim, you know these people—you work with them, you live next door to them, you put them up in a spare bedroom over the holidays.

Adding to Bunyan's appeal is his treatment of pilgrimage as a metaphor for life. His tale isn't simply about a hallucinatory hike to a shining city where those few admitted receive a gold harp at the gate (though Bunyan's belief in such a place was literal, right down to the harps). It's also about our universal need to find the right way in life, to strive for something more—to be better people, to make a difference in the world, to hope no one looks too closely at our tax returns. Our beliefs and goals may differ, and the trials we face may vary, but we can all identify with Christian when, at the outset of his quest, he examines his life and cries, "What shall I do?"

When I am confronted with that question, I stare into the dark abyss (or, more likely, a tumbler of Glenlivet) for a couple of days until the panic subsides. Then I ask myself another question: "Well, what do other people do?" This accomplishes two things. First, it takes the existential heat off me. Second, it forces me off my duff and out into the real world, where I can indulge my favorite pastime—watching other people. Aside from its entertainment value, observing others can tell us something revealing about ourselves, even if only to clarify who or what we are not, or to illuminate a set of beliefs to which, we can then safely say, we do or do not subscribe.

For several years now, I've made exploring what others believe, and writing about how their religious views shape their lives, something of a personal quest. The result is this book. Despite its similarities to *Pilgrim's Progress*, the differences are much more obvious. For one thing, the people in this book are real. Bunyan created characters that represent types and attitudes, and he used them to advance the Puritan doctrine of conversion. My book does not have a theological agenda per se because, unlike Bunyan, I've yet to find the one true path.

In other words, whereas Bunyan wrote with an all-consuming fire of conviction, I write out of curiosity—the sheer delight of learning what makes other people tick. For example, it was with genuine awe that I went to visit Pete Halvorson, a man who, practicing the ancient art of trepanation, drilled a hole in his skull to make himself permanently happy. Similarly, it was with slack-jawed wonder that I watched Omega and Apocalypse, headliners with the Christian Wrestling Federation, open up a can of whup ass in order to "spread the good news of Jesus Christ."

In a sense, this book is an inversion of Bunyan's. Whereas Christian hazards a world full of nonbelievers, I encounter people who are nothing if not true believers. Yet, like Christian on his journey to the Celestial City, I'm never sure who awaits me around the next bend, or what I might find in the cities and burgs that lie ahead. When I went, for example, to meet the women who run Dying-to-Get-In, a company specializing in faux funerals, I did not expect to find myself laid out in a pink coffin, cruising down crowded Long Island streets in the back of a flamingo pink hearse.

Indeed, every pilgrimage is fraught with peril. But whereas Christian lamented, "What shall I do to be saved?" I was inclined to wail, during one foolhardy experiment, "How can I pose as a street preacher in Times Square, damning perfect strangers to hell, and still get back home with my hide intact, preferably in time for dinner?"

I've organized my stream of adventures according to the places featured in *Pilgrim's Progress*—the City of Destruction, Vanity Fair, the Slough of Despond, et cetera. The rationale behind my groupings is in most cases clear. All the pieces that fall under Vanity Fair, for instance, deal in some way with, well, vanity or the marketplace, whether it's Jerry Falwell hawking videotapes on an infomercial, the Christian Booksellers Association's annual convention, or an itinerant preacher named Whatsyourname, who was ignored by the masses until he made himself look a lot like Jesus.

Also included under Vanity Fair, however, is "The Saint of Sin City," a story about Charlie Bolin, a salt-of-the-earth guy who happens to be the only full-time chaplain on the payroll of a Las Vegas casino. (Hey, how can you have a Vegas story, complete with topless dancers, and not stick it in Vanity Fair?) As another nod to Bunyan's book, which was written in the form of a dream, I've included a section called A Pilgrim's Dreams, which features parodies and other flights of fancy. For the final chapter, I became an actual pilgrim—or, depending on your perspective, a grimy, panting metaphor—as I walked the ancient, five-hundred-mile pilgrimage route to Santiago de Compostela, Spain.

But, in a way, it doesn't matter that much how I've ordered this book. The events in *Pilgrim's Progress* aren't really sequential or geographical; they're psychological. That's why Christian, after traveling a long distance to Vanity Fair, as one scholar says, winds up back at the City of Destruction, where he started, though he doesn't realize it.

I don't know about you, reader, but I personally draw some hope from the thought that one of literature's most devout and determined pilgrims actually went in circles.

The City of Destruction

Then Apollyon, espying his opportunity, began to gather up close to Christian, and wrestling with him, gave him a dreadful fall; and with that Christian's sword flew out of his hand. Then said Apollyon, "I am sure of thee now," and with that he had almost pressed him to death, so that Christian began to despair of life. *

---

* A note to *Progress* purists: No, I'm not trying to pull the wool over your eyes. True, this fight scene actually happened in the Valley of Humiliation. But *you* try finding a decent epigraph among Bunyan's references to the City of Destruction.

God's Smackdown

The teenage boys sitting in the back row in the Lititz Community Center, in Lititz, Pennsylvania, a small town east of Harrisburg, kept snorting dismissively at the spiritual battle unfolding before our eyes. In a ring set up in the middle of a couple hundred folding chairs, Omega, a 215-pounder who wrestles in the name of the Lord, propped himself up on the ropes and landed both feet in the face of Big Tim Storm, knocking him to the mat. Omega pounced and pummeled Big Tim with blows to the chest and throat. The teenagers looked like they'd rather be behind the 7-Eleven smoking cigarettes.

But Big Tim, a long-haired, sweaty human wrecking machine at six-foot-three and 260 pounds, has his own yen for Jesus and, grabbing his "rag doll pansy" of an opponent, flung him out of the ring. By the time he'd foot-stomped Omega's head a dozen times, the ten-year-olds a few rows up were counting each blow aloud. As Big Tim, exulting in his win, strutted and bellowed "shut up" to the kids' boos and at the blue-haired lady hissing and giving him a thumbs-down, his real accomplishment was whipping up the listless Lititz crowd.

His ring victory, a wrestler named Apocalypse later pointed out, really belonged not to Big Tim but to the big man upstairs: "We come out here and beat each other up every night for one reason and one reason only," Apocalypse told the crowd. "To spread the good news of Jesus Christ!"

Far from the World Wrestling Federation's packed arenas and vulgarian displays is the Christian Wrestling Federation, the nation's first and only full-time wrestling ministry. Since 2000, the Texas-based group has performed at scores of church-sponsored events across the country. (In Lititz, the wrestlers were invited by a local United Methodist church, which fed and housed them.) The CWF is "a non-profit organization," its website explains, "that hopes to express the love of God in a new and dynamic way."

Each show consists of four or five no-holds-barred matches, rife with taunts, hair pulls, and smackdowns, but decorously free of the coarse language and bikini-clad women prevalent in that other professional wrestling organization, the stuff you see on big-time cable stations. True, the Christian Wrestlers, like their secular peers, are big guys with big mouths who, except for the spandex and knee pads, look like extras in a prison film. But in the CWF the music that blasts between matches is Christian rock. Inscribed on the sides of the ring is the group's mission verse: "Finally, be strong in the Lord and in His power. Ephesians 6:10." Every show ends in prayer.

The founder of CWF, Rob Vaughn, got the inspiration for Christian wrestling in 1999. A thirty-three-year-old former arena football coach and an ordained Baptist minister, Vaughn—whose ring name is Jesus Freak—had briefly wrestled on an independent circuit in Texas.

He witnessed things he did not like. "It was a bad scene," said Vaughn. "Guys drinking and smoking pot in the locker room, and everybody out for himself. Nobody wants to get beat or upstaged. There's lots of swearing and extreme violence, people throwing tables and chairs, blood everywhere. Plus, there are half-dressed women parading around. And I thought, Does the five-year-old in the front row really need to see all this? It wasn't anything that I, as a Christian, wanted to be a part of anymore."

But just as Vaughn was about to hang up his boots, a minister friend in San Antonio had an idea. "He said, 'Why don't you create a wrestling ministry?'" Vaughn recalled. "After a month of intense prayer, I decided to pursue it."

Vaughn registered the CWF name and spent eight months getting funding from friends and churches, locating a training ring, and opening an office in Rockwall, a suburb east of Dallas. To find wrestlers, he sent three thousand flyers to area churches, though he discovered a few born-again bashers in unlikely places. "I went to see an independent show held in a bar," Vaughn said. "In the first match there was a guy named the Saint, and he was introduced with a Christian rock song. His wrestling was good, clean action, so afterward I went up to him and learned he's a pastor at a church in Fort Worth!" The Saint joined the CWF the next week.

The ministering is plentifully mixed in with the wrestling. Twice during each show a wrestler shares his faith with the crowd. At intermission in Lititz, a wrestler named Jonah spoke about temptation. "What is temptation?" he asked, pacing the ring. "You walk into a store and see something you want, but you don't have any money. You take it anyway. *That* is temptation for material objects! You're at a bar, throwing back some brewskis, and people are startin' to like ya because you're mister funny man, dancin' around. *That* is temptation for social acceptance!"

At the end of the evening, Apocalypse made a distinction between accepting Jesus with your heart and accepting him with your head. For years, Apocalypse went to church every Sunday and every Wednesday night. He led his youth group and memorized Scripture. "I knew all the right answers, but I didn't *know* all the right answers," he said. "Like many of you here, I was wearing a mask. And if you're wearing a mask, you have to seriously question whether you're going to heaven or hell if you were to die tonight."

After praying the "sinner's prayer"—"all you have to do is ask Jesus into your heart and he will come"—Apocalypse gave the altar call, or "ring call," if you will. Audience members who accepted Jesus were invited down front to speak privately and pray with a wrestler about their life-altering decision. Three bewildered-looking teenage girls stepped forward. "Man, that's awesome," Apocalypse said. "Everybody give 'em a hand!"

The matches themselves aren't very different from those of the WWF. While anarchic violence reigns at some point in each match, all pro wrestling is a morality play. The crowd is there to watch the good guys punish the bad guys, and most often they go home happy. In Christian wrestling, the bad guys are just as likely to end the night testifying as the good guys. It's a close copy of the real thing, but the moral takes precedence over the characters.

"Basically, every show tells a story," said Vaughn. "We present a gospel message through wrestling and Scripture. For example, a wrestler may lose the battle in the ring one night. That's the way it is in real life—we lose battles. But with Jesus Christ as our lord and savior, we can come back and win the war! Wrestling is so popular with kids these days," he added, "it's a great way to draw them to Jesus."

Of the federation's fifteen wrestlers, five are ordained ministers and several teach Sunday school. Many of their names are inspired by the Bible—Jonah, Angel, Martyr. "Each guy picks his own name," said Vaughn. "Some aren't biblical at all, like Big Tim Storm or the New York Nightmare, but suit the wrestler's personality. I chose Jesus Freak because I reckoned there's a lot of freaks out there, and if I'm going to be a freak for anything, I'm going to be a freak for Jesus."

When they're not on the road, the wrestlers train three nights a week at a warehouse in the Fort Worth area and attend a mandatory weekly Bible study. The punishing nature of the ministry takes a toll; the troupe had recently taken a month off to heal. "We were so banged up," Vaughn said. "We had neck problems, back problems, shoulder problems. Broken noses and broken ribs. In Arizona, Jonah broke his wrist. Fortunately, we have a chiropractor in Dallas who treats us for free. That's his ministry to us."

"The Bible talks about what is a reasonable sacrifice," Big Tim Storm, a.k.a. Tim Scoggins, explained as he sipped bottled water after the show. "We believe the physical sacrifices we make are reasonable. I've had torn ACLs, no cartilage in my knee. I've had concussions. You name it. But that's what this is all about. We accept the risks, just as you accept the risk every time you cross the street."

Scoggins estimated that he flies through the air and lands flat on his back roughly thirty times a night. "When we step into the ring, we have to give it one hundred percent," he said, "because our commitment, our sacrifice, has to be pure. And if just one person accepts Jesus, then it's all worth it."

The visit to Lititz drew roughly sixty to a hundred attendees, mostly church kids and their friends. The next stop was the fifteenth annual Kingdom Bound Christian Festival, at Six Flags in Darien Center, New York, which draws some sixty thousand faithful. It was easily the CWF's biggest event so far.

Vaughn said the CWF has been on a roll since the group was featured on *CBS News Sunday Morning*. The next day Vaughn received a flood of calls and e-mails, including one from a real-estate agent in Florida. "He said, 'I'm a Christian, and I hate wrestling,'" Vaughn recalled, "'but, man, what you guys are doing is unique. I saw that you're pulling a U-Haul, and I feel the Lord is leading me to help you guys out. Go pick out a trailer, and I'll buy it for you.' So we picked out the perfect trailer, and he sent us a check."

As Vaughn sees it, the future is in God's hands. "Basically, we are surviving on no budget," he said. "We don't have an athletic shoe company sponsoring us. But somehow we manage to pay our bills every month. God continues to bless us, sending us people willing to help.

"Of course, all this could end tomorrow," he said. "And if so, it's been a great run. We've seen hundreds of people get saved. But as long as the Lord continues to support us, and we're willing and able, we'll go wherever he leads us.

"We kind of think of ourselves in terms of Jesus' disciples—just ordinary men who did extraordinary things."

A Tree Stand Close to Heaven

I don't typically buy my books in gas stations. But as I waited to pay for a pit stop in rural Pennsylvania, one book on the register rack leapt out at me—*With God on a Deer Hunt*, by Steve Chapman.

In my suburb, we have a "deer problem." Letters in the local papers complain about these "rodents" eating our shrubs and blocking our streets. Loosening residential hunting laws is often proposed as the best solution for curbing the rogue deer's numbers. Others argue that killing enough deer to make a difference would mean turning my 'burb into a war zone.

With God on a Deer Hunt looked like it might have some answers. As a rule, I try not to kill animals. I brake for chipmunks, and I slow down if I spot a deer even near the road. If I find a spider in my house, I release it outside. Hell, why not? Opening the door and setting a spider on a bush is just not as inconvenient as it might sound. Could there be biblical justification for killing the deer?

I've since learned that this isn't a crazy notion. According to "Should We Hunt?" on the Christian Bowhunters' website (www.christianbowhunters.org), God clearly permits hunting in Genesis 27:3 and Leviticus 17:13. We may hunt animals, the bowhunters argue further, because animals are not "rational, moral, eternal bound beings." Those who disagree are "fully given over to the oriental religions and have sealed their fate to hell by the denial of sinful man, a holy, justice seeking God, a condescending Savior, a resurrected Christ and life with Jesus forever."

When heads are cooler, the Christian Bowhunters concede that, unlike as in ancient days, we no longer need to hunt to survive. Survival, however, is defined in many ways: In suburbia, the mandate to develop more malls is akin to survival.

Chapman's book, it turned out, is not about controlling the deer population. Nor, unlike many of my neighbors, does Chapman dismiss deer as "varmints." If anything, he reveres the animals for their grace, beauty, and intelligence. At the mere sight of a deer, he says, "my nerves tend to turn into a bowl of shaky Jell-O."

Nevertheless, he doesn't address what we might think about killing deer. Each chapter offers Scripture and a brief hunting anecdote, which, according to the back cover, celebrates "the excitement of matching wits with the elusive whitetail and the breathtaking joy of entering God's presence." It hadn't occurred to me that dressing up in camouflage and chasing God's creation through the woods with a high-powered rifle could serve as a way of "drawing near to the Lord."

Strictly speaking, Chapman doesn't draw near to the Lord just by killing. In fact, he doesn't spend a lot of his time in the woods actually shooting deer. Most of his time is consumed sitting in trees *waiting* to kill deer. It's during these long, lonely stretches that he does the bulk of his theological musing. For example, in Chapter 3, "The Slap," he recalls a day he sat in a tree swatting mosquitoes. He got so mad at the insects that he hauled off and smashed one against his face. He killed the bug, all right, but, he recounts, "I also managed to seriously rattle my own cage." The pain evoked his wife's story about a guy who bullied her in high school. One day she smacked her antagonist across the face. "The sound of the hand-on-cheek explosion was deafening," he writes. "The sudden noise of teeth banging violently against one another was excruciating to hear. The deed was done." The result of which was that the bully never bothered her again.

Chapman's point? His wife's slap illustrates Psalm 3:7— "Arise, O Lord; save me, O my God! For you have smitten all my enemies on the cheek; You have shattered the teeth of the wicked."

In fact, Chapman kills many more mosquitoes while hunting than he does deer. In Chapter 25, "Attacked!" he recalls how he was once so beset by "pesky, pistol-packin' skeeters" that he raced back to camp to don his "armor"—an extra shirt, a second pair of pants, two pairs of gloves, and an additional face mask. Though he felt like he "was hunting in a sleeping bag inside a sauna," he managed to shoot a mule deer. "It was some of the best meat I've ever eaten," he writes, "because I won the 'war'" against the mosquitoes. This tale sheds new light on Ephesians 6:11: "Put on the full armor of God."

Other spiritual lessons Chapman gleaned while hunting:

- The apples he uses to entice deer into shooting range deposit seeds in the soil that will bring forth more apple trees. (Genesis 1:12)

- Gazing intently in the woods for deer is similar to the way we should examine Scripture for God's truths. (James 1:25)
- If your tree stand is too comfortable, you might drift off to sleep and fall out of the tree. Similarly, God does not want us to grow complacent. (Deuteronomy 8:11–14)
- Even if you have a terrible voice, no one will hear you sing in your tree stand except God, whose "concern is 'our hearts . . . not the *Billboard* charts.'" (Psalm 13:6)
- Just as we paralyze deer with the headlights of our cars, so does God shine the light of his countenance upon us. (Psalm 4:6)

For all of Chapman's preaching, he never addresses whether actually killing the deer would bother God. As a moral guide, Chapman is on a par with Ted Nugent, the rock star, NRA board member, and outdoorsman extraordinaire. In his *New York Times* bestseller, *God, Guns, & Rock 'n' Roll*, Nugent makes it clear that killing animals is for him a deeply religious experience. "As the arrow comes back," he writes, "I slowly repeat, 'In the name of the Father, and of the Son, and of the Holy Spirit,' then, as my eyes lock on his pump-station entrance rib, the arrow is gone at 'Amen!'"

There are no lessons for us here, beyond the unambiguous spiritual rapture of killing itself. In the section "The Ballistics of Spirituality—You Can't Grill It 'Til You Kill It," Nugent explains: "Those of us who are driven to participate in as many predator dawns as possible are baptized over and over, again and again, by the hand of God and His stunning, mystical creation." Hunting is "a spiritual orgasm." And it's legal.

God's endorsement of hunting is incontrovertible in Nugent's mind. In the chapter "My Son, the Pigkiller—How Proud Can a Dad Get?" he reasons: "If God didn't want us to eat pork why would He have put all that meat on pigs and dealt with their stinking porcine misbehavior on Noah's ark?" One could counter that just because God put meat on Nugent's bones, that doesn't necessarily mean God wants us to flame-broil "Ol' Hunka Ted." Then again, who knows? One of the epigraphs Nuge selected for his book is Genesis 9:3: "Every moving thing that liveth shall be meat for you."

Half the pleasure of Nugent's book is its flat-out, unabashed celebration of guns—"I love guns. The more, the better. The more ammo, the better" he gushes. And hunting—"There are more than four million whitetail deer in Texas, and I'm out to find 'em all." But for all his goofy bravado, Nugent does what Chapman never does—slips in some introspection about hunting, or at least pauses to dismiss it: "We are the only predators," he says, "who hit the hay each night with our bubbling conscience."

Fierce Animals

There's at least one drawback to being an ancient culture that had no written language and didn't build pyramids: You give folks in the future lots of room to think whatever they want about you. Or so I mused at the Georgia Museum of Art, at the University of Georgia in Athens, as I listened to college students, all baggy pants, Birkenstocks, and body piercings, discuss a case of pottery in *Gold, Jade, Forests: Costa Rica,* an exhibition of pre-Columbian art that toured museums across the United States.

"That vase, dudes," said Nose Ring. "What purity."

"Their art shows how much the indigenous peoples communed with nature," added Six-Inch Goatee. "If only we had a shred of their ecological awareness . . ."

"Yeah," said Yin-Yang Tattoo, "and then Western, quote unquote, civilization took over."

Their comments ran like this for more than an hour. What were they talking about? As I toured the exhibit, I was thinking about the National Football League—the Eagles, the Falcons, the Seahawks. The Ravens, the Bears, the Lions. And what do a bunch of guys who pose as fierce animals and bruise each other to win trophies have to do with pre-Columbian art?

Quite a bit, actually.

There were 142 objects in this show, and the lion's share depicted, well, fierce animals.

Consider the clay ocelot. The creature stands on its hind legs, ears back and eyes ablaze; its bared fangs drip the blood of its prey. Or the lurid gold cat pendant. Crouched for the kill, flashing razor-sharp teeth, this highly stylized form could be a jaguar. With its simple design, it could also pass muster as an emblem for a team in the NFL like, say, the Jacksonville Jaguars.

But don't take my word for it. Ask E. Michael Whittington, curator of pre-Columbian and African art at the Mint Museum of Art in Charlotte, North Carolina. He's the one who got me thinking in terms of pigskin.

"Cultures have always identified with animals, particularly predators," Whittington told me. "The jaguar was the dominant predator in much of the pre-Columbian world, so it's prevalent in their art. Same thing today. Go to any football game—and I've got slides to back this up—and you'll see people with their faces painted up like jaguars or panthers.

"They may not understand why they do this, but I do."

I do, too—Budweiser. "Why?" I asked.

"They're assuming the qualities of ferocity they hope their team will emulate," he said. "What happened in these pre-Columbian societies was much more dramatic. The religious practitioners, or shamans, who acted as intermediaries between the supernatural and human worlds, believed they could actually transform into jaguars and roam the forest floor.

"The shamans," he continued, "took hallucinogenic substances to achieve an altered state of awareness, during which they believed their spirits flew from their bodies to become jaguars."

So maybe beer wasn't that far off after all.

I certainly found festivity in the gold pieces that depicted human-animal transformations. Men with faces of monkeys, jaguars, and lizards danced and played musical instruments. Some were simple, naked forms; others were clad in ceremonial garb, including ornate headdresses, considered awards for exploits in battle. One pendant, a human with the mask of a harpy eagle, had wings that moved, simulating flight. The figures seemed fit to burst with life and vitality, the exuberance of ritual accented by the shimmer of gold.

Unlike the beauty of these objects, however, their significance was not always self-evident. For instance, I was plain stumped by the jade cat that has a bird's head for a rump.

Fortunately, the exhibition catalog helped me decipher this. Sort of. It has to do with pre-Columbian societies' religious beliefs, which stem from their need to understand and control their environment. They divided the world into three mythological zones—land, sky, and water—and they revered animals for the ways they inhabited these zones. Jaguars and snakes possess unique skills for surviving on land, as do owls and macaws in the sky, and sharks and lobsters in water.

Naturally, these societies ascribed special significance to animals that lorded over two or more realms, such as monkeys, which both walked on land and climbed trees, and crocodiles, which both crawled and swam. So when I saw a jade bat with crocodile heads for wings, it made perfect sense to me. This creature can fly, crawl, and swim. It dwells in all three zones, and might just be able to transport the souls of the dead to the next world.

Still, I couldn't figure out that cat with a bird butt. (Picture Sylvester and Tweety as Siamese twins and I think you catch my drift.)

But that was the least of my concerns as my museum visit drew to a close. As I left the exhibit, Nose Ring and company joined me in the elevator, where they continued their ponderings. It seemed they'd learned "lessons" from the pre-Columbians about ecology and harmony. I wanted to ask if they'd noticed the mace heads and the ocelot's bloodlust. But I didn't. I was too guilt-ridden that I didn't learn such lessons myself.

Even the Georgia Museum of Art's literature claimed that the exhibition focused on "the unique and harmonious relationship between man and nature in [Costa Rica]." Missed that, too. Sure, I was amazed by pre-Columbian artistic sophistication and intellectual curiosity. But from what I saw in their art, these folks may have viewed nature much as we, sometimes for better but mostly for worse, do today—as a resource that fulfills our basic needs.

Later, I explained my quandary to Michael Whittington.

"Well, it's self-evident that ancient peoples were in touch with their environment," he said. "But it's also a highly romanticized notion, because many were not forest-dwelling utopians who lived in complete harmony with nature. In fact, there's a lot of evidence that suggests that many ancient peoples completely deforested their landscape. This often got them in great ecological trouble, and eventually led to their demise.

"That," he said, "is the lesson."

Vanity Fair

*When they were got out of the wilderness they presently
saw a town before them, and the name of that town is
Vanity; and at that town there is a fair kept called
Vanity-Fair. . . . At this Fair are all such merchandise
sold as houses, lands, trades, places, honours, prefer-
ments, titles, countries, kingdoms, lusts, pleasures, and
delights of all sorts.*

Where the Boys Aren't

"What are you doing at a spa?"

This was my father speaking. I was on the phone from Canyon Ranch, a health resort in the Berkshires. "Lots of things," I told him. "I just had a shiatsu massage."

"From a man or a woman?" he asked.

"A man."

Dead silence. I knew exactly what he was thinking. My father is of that generation for whom the word *massage* means a seedy room drenched in red light and a wisp of an Asian girl. Finally I said, "I don't consider massage a . . . sexual experience."

"Yeah," my father said, "but that doesn't mean he doesn't."

I thought better of my temptation to explain further that Canyon Ranch is a destination that makes frank use of terms such as *holistic* and *wellness*. Back in his day, in the late fifties and early sixties, my father, too, went to the Berkshires to unwind. He and his buddies stayed at a place called Eastover, remarkable for its Civil War motif. The American Heritage Room, an underground museum filled with artifacts that include a Gatling gun, anchors an array of cottages named Lee, Grant, and Jeb Stuart. The indoor pool features portholes for those who enjoy watching people swim. "It's a real hot spot for swinging singles," a local told me when I asked him about Eastover, "where they still drink and dance till dawn." Canyon Ranch, by contrast, beckons to those who, like me, read too many magazines that, come winter, begin running health and fitness articles that underscore just how short we fall in the body-mind-spirit department. "In addition to the finest in spa activities, programs and services," the spa's brochure reads, "we also focus on nutrition, preventive medicine, women's health issues, spiritual awareness, exercise and the potential for behavioral change."

There are few men at Canyon Ranch, much less pasty-white, thirtysomething guys like me. I visited the first week in March, and the majority of guests were wealthy, middle-aged women from New York and New Jersey. On my first day, I almost asked at guest services if perhaps I'd booked my stay during a women's retreat. My daily abs class consisted of me and twenty-five women squatting on exercise balls. The men's stretch class was two other guys and me, plus a staff member limbering up on his break. It's the type of place where my masculinity got an abrupt boost when a woman at dinner reported seeing James Taylor, a Ranch regular, on the treadmill, and the other women at the table cooed.

The absence of men is a bit puzzling. Men are as susceptible as women to the status, if not the holistic pampering, Canyon Ranch confers. An off-season stay starts at $1,460 for three nights and goes up to $3,580 for a seven-night package for an individual. Every year the Berkshire Canyon Ranch vies with its sister in Tucson, Arizona, for *Condé Nast Traveler*'s readers' choice award as best spa in the world. The resort, on 120 wooded acres in Lenox, Massachusetts, offers more than forty fitness activities and seventy-five health and healing consultations daily. The staff-to-guest ratio is three to one, and the guest capacity is 240. Canyon Ranch has a 100,000-square-foot spa complex, and the first thing you see as you drive past the gate is the spa's architectural center-piece—Bellefontaine, a mansion built by a robber baron in 1897 and patterned after Louis XV's Petit Trianon in Versailles.

Men certainly shouldn't object to the food. A far cry from rabbit pellets, meals at Canyon Ranch include healthy gourmet dishes ranging from tasty pizzas and chilis to satisfying portions of lamb and whole lobsters. And no matter how decadent the entrée may sound—chicken with portobello and saffron cream sauce over pasta, for example—each dish usually contains between 300 and 500 calories. Desserts include cheesecake and hot-fudge sundaes. And the kitchen welcomes special requests. At my first meal, I asked if some-one could make me a mixed-vegetable juice, which was not offered on the menu. "Of course," the waitress said. "And if you'd like, we could note to bring you one with each meal." I told her I'd take one glass per day at lunch, and I never men-tioned it again. The juice automatically appeared with my entrée every afternoon.

So were women applauding my "brave decision" to go there? "I've tried to get my husband to come for years," one told me as we trotted on adjacent treadmills. "But he'd rather go on a golf vacation and smoke cigars." Another woman said that her husband thought Canyon Ranch was "too girlie," and that he "doesn't like to be pampered."

Perhaps men don't realize there is a manly way to go about a spa like Canyon Ranch: Extreme Pampering. I attacked the ranch as I imagined George Patton would have. I signed up for at least one fifty-minute massage per day, alternating Swedish with shiatsu. I had two hypnotherapy sessions, which would maximize my mental and physical relaxation and help me achieve my fitness goals. I tried acupuncture and, for the heck of it, had an astrology and tarot-card reading. (The news was all good, even though most of my cards depicted ominous stones or swords.)

I tried things I thought wouldn't appeal to me—Austrian mud therapy, for instance. I was painted head to toe with European Moor Mud while my face and feet were massaged. Then I was wrapped in plastic and left under a heat lamp so that minerals released from the mud would help rid my body of toxins. This forty-five-minute treatment turned out to be an ingenious form of torture. My arms immobile at my sides, I felt like a Saran-wrapped mummy. Halfway through, sweat started dripping into my ears. Finally, I couldn't take the itching any longer and shouted for the therapist to come clean my ears out with a towel. I was mollified only when, after a thorough shower, I was covered with an application of body milk.

You can do whatever you want with your time at Canyon Ranch. Program coordinators will design a schedule tailored to your goals, or, as I did, you may create your own program. Every day, in addition to two or three exercise classes— yoga, stretch, aerobics—I ran eight miles on the treadmill and worked out with weights for an hour. After dinner, I would attend one of the many health and nutrition talks.

I confess I did skip the Wild Woman Pack Chat ("Come discover the wild woman inside you!"). I also had a night off when, perplexingly, "Healing with Chinese Herbs" was "cancelled due to an illness."

Truth be told, Canyon Ranch was my wife's idea. Apparently, I was showing signs of cabin fever. "Why don't you get away and indulge yourself a bit?" she suggested, handing me a spa guide. "Canyon Ranch has all sorts of fitness stuff you like, but don't just work out. Get pampered, too."

My new rule of thumb is: A massage goes a very long way. On my last day there, I scheduled a hundred-minute therapy called Euphoria for noon. If my visit to Canyon Ranch could be likened to a fireworks display, Euphoria was the grand finale.

Here's what you get: After a shower, you are deposited on a table in a candlelit room where soft music is playing. Your face is wrapped in warm towels that have been dipped in sage oil. Then comes an aromatherapy scalp massage with rose geranium oil, followed by a warm botanical body mask. Once you're gently buffed clean, you soak in a hot tub scented with grapefruit oil. Then you're back on the table for a Swedish massage using rich Ayurvedic oils. The woman who performed all this on me said she sees at most one or two men a month for the treatment. I mumbled something back to the effect that other men have no idea what they are missing.

But here's the rub. I had also recklessly scheduled a Swedish massage for 5:00. Stumbling into my Swedish appointment still slack-jawed and cross-eyed from Euphoria, I wanted to tell the masseur to wait in the hall while I spent the session napping. Instead, I just let the guy knead away at muscles he couldn't have made looser if he pounded them with a meat tenderizer.

While social scientists work on the mystery of why more men don't go to Canyon Ranch, I'll be happy to return some-day and have the men's areas all to myself. Not once in my visit did I have to share a whirlpool, sauna, or steam room. The only depressing thing for me were the men's program trainers, who were always available to play tennis or lift weights. Whenever they saw me coming, they'd shout, "Hey, want to shoot some hoops? Go cross-country skiing? Do some snowshoeing?"

I know what my father would tell them. Take a couple hours off, guys, and go have a few drinks at Eastover.

All the Luck in the World

Everyone has a system when it comes to the lottery. Some people like to play their birth date, or their children's ages. Others consult their astrological chart. I took another tack and drove to Beaver Meadows, Pennsylvania. At Bernie's Variety Mart, an undistinguished drive-up store on the main road to Hazleton, between Scranton and Allentown, I bought a half dozen Super 6 tickets. According to the state of Pennsylvania, my odds of winning that night's $14 million prize were pathetic: 1 in 39,959,158. What the lottery didn't factor in was the man who'd be picking the numbers—Joe Hornick, Sr., holder of perhaps the luckiest lottery-winning streak ever.

Since 1989 Hornick, a sixty-seven-year-old Catholic and semiretired owner of a home-heating-oil business, has hit four jackpots—three with tickets from Bernie's Variety Mart—for a total of almost $3 million. Joe's first and biggest win, a $2.5 million Super 7 in 1989, defied 6-million-to-1 odds. Joe had a banner year in 2001. In June, the Cash 5 paid him $206,217. Three weeks later, still waiting for his previous check, Joe hit the Cash 5 again, for $71,037. The odds of winning the Cash 5 just once are 1 in 575,757. Joe has now hit it three times. (In 1997, he struck for $68,000.) Oh, and that April, Joe asked his nephew to buy him a ticket in Florida while there on business. Joe won $6,673.

Joe, who still plays the lottery daily, rarely spends more than forty dollars a week on tickets.

In his 1988 book, *Innumeracy: Mathematical Illiteracy and Its Consequences,* John Allen Paulos calculates that choosing just six numbers from 1 to 40, a person can come up with 3,838,380 possible combinations—seemingly an abstract task but not to the millions who play state-sponsored lotteries every week. This means the odds of picking a winning six are staggeringly poor, and get worse with every additional number. Paulos goes on to note that someone, however improbably, does win, and often. But what are the odds that the winner will be the same guy, so many times?

"A math professor once calculated the odds of all my wins," Joe tells me, his voice booming over the phone after, much to my surprise, I found him listed in the phone book. "And he said it'd be like the same person getting struck by lightning six hundred times!"

Some wish lightning *would* strike Joe. When asked to what he attributed his luck, Joe used to claim it was "divine intervention." He explained to the *Today* show host Matt Lauer, after his second jackpot that summer, "I've got the Lord on my side." The response of the righteous was swift and fierce. "I got a flood of calls and letters," says Joe, a stocky, silver-haired guy who could be played by Charles Durning at top volume. "People telling me I'm going to hell for using God to win the lottery."

Add to his bum rap that Joe once picked some of his winning numbers from his church bulletin—Scripture verses in

Jeremiah. "Boy, the flak I got!" he says. "People calling me an immoral blasphemer for using the Bible like that. Some even said God should strike me dead!"

But Dolly, Joe's wife of forty-six years, tells me later, over coffee in the Hornicks' kitchen, that the reactionaries miss the point. "Joe picking those numbers from the bulletin is no different than the time he got the numbers off an aftershave bottle," she says. "Or when he played four digits in our zip code—and hit 'em."

"I got tired of the repercussions of mentioning God," says Hornick. "Now I just tell them it's luck—luck, luck, luck!" he says, pounding the table.

That doesn't keep strangers from treating Hornick like a lightning rod. They approach him on the street and ask to rub him for luck—"like I'm the Holy Grail or a wooden Indian," he says.

Ha, you say. But two weeks before my pilgrimage to his house, Hornick's friend Jerry asked to rub Joe for luck. "So I says, 'Go ahead,' and bent over," says Joe, demonstrating the pose. "He smacked me on the rear, and that night he hit four numbers for $414." When Jerry called Joe with the good news, he asked Joe to wish him more luck, so he did. That night Jerry hit the daily number twice for $1,000. "He was so bent out of shape on the phone you'd think he won a million." Joe told Jerry to brace himself; luck comes in threes: The following Tuesday, Jerry hit for $313.

In the Hornicks' hometown of Coxeville, a small, predominantly Catholic working-class town next to Beaver Meadows, faith looms large. The hand of God, not random chance, is generally perceived as determining daily life. At a neighbor's wedding after Joe's first big win, the priest's talk took an odd turn. "He looked straight at us," Dolly says, "and said, 'When you think you're the reason something good has happened to you, just remember, you didn't do anything at all. God did it for you!' Everyone was annoyed he said that to us—during a wedding!"

The problem Joe's good fortune presents to the griping faithful seems to come down to this: If there are no accidents in life, and God orchestrates every event, then Joe's winnings must be divinely ordained. But this, of course, raises the unsettling question, "Why him, and why not me or any other hardworking, decent person I know?" On the other hand, his critics may conclude that God had nothing to do with Joe's winnings. But this broaches what is for most of them an equally disturbing prospect—that life is teeming with accidents. (It's not surprising that Joe doesn't receive angry mail from atheists or agnostics.)

Hornick's own priest takes a lighter view. He cracked that their house had once been a stable, and that Joe must have stepped in a horse pie, which according to an old superstition brings luck.

For many, the lure of a jackpot is irresistible, making state lotteries a $35-billion-a-year industry. According to a report by the National Gambling Impact Study Commission, appointed by Congress in 1999, almost 6 million Americans are either compulsive or problem gamblers, and another 15 million gamble beyond their means. And the people most addicted to gambling tend to be those who can least afford to lose— the less educated and the poor. People who live in the poorest areas of New Jersey, a *New York Times* article reported, spend more than five times as much of their income on lottery tickets as do people who live in the state's wealthiest areas. Those who blow their paychecks on lottery tickets are motivated by desperation and wishful thinking: *Against the odds, I'm going to win a jackpot, solve all my problems, and start a new life.*

Joe claims his wins have "not changed my life one iota." He lives in the same modest three-family house where he was born. Cousins and nieces live there too, as well as his two sons and six grandchildren. Rising beyond Joe's backyard is a mountain of shale several stories tall, refuse from what was once a coal mine. He still drives the Subaru he owned before he started hitting it big.

When I appeared to interview Joe, he reached into a bag and offered me a fast-food hamburger. "Hell, I don't need surf 'n' turf," he said later, working on some fries. "I'm happy with peanut butter and jelly and McDonald's."

"He's being humble when he chalks it up to luck," says Joe Jr. (whose own lottery winnings over twenty years total forty dollars). "He's worked hard all his life, and he's been very kind to people. Even before he won the lottery, he's always given money to the community, and he's never wanted to be recognized for it. I believe he's being rewarded for the way he's lived his life. If you're religious, you might call that God."

If so, God doesn't play only lotto. After appearing on *Today,* Joe took his cousin to Atlantic City to celebrate. Joe played the slots and went home $2,200 richer. Two weeks later he returned to Atlantic City and came out $2,600 ahead. "But that's nothing!" he barks, leaning across the table to swat me on the shoulder. "Two years ago Dolly won $9,970 off one pull at Bally's. Four years before that, she won $10,700 off a quarter at the Sands, went right next door to Bally's and won $2,000!"

Joe points out that his winnings don't go as far as most people think. For starters, he still has to work. After taxes, the annuity from his $2.5 million winner comes to $85,000. He passes much of that on to relatives. "I sent my grandkids through private Catholic school, all six of them," he says. "The oldest one's in college. They all had braces, at $5,000 each. My grandson's car just got out of the garage. The bill's $184, and I have to pay it. This year was different because I won two other jackpots, but by the time April comes, I usually need a little luck."

It's odd to hear a lottery prodigy wishing for more luck. But at one point he leaves the kitchen and comes back with a stack of letters—hard luck stories from around the world asking for handouts. One, written in German, included a doctor's diagnosis. A letter from upstate New York, accompanied by a program from a memorial service, read: "I too play the lottery trying to keep our head over the water. I won't give up. I can't. I believe prayer changes things . . . and when you said only God knows about your future winnings, I hope God knows when me and my mother will one day be blessed." Joe does not answer these letters.

Nonetheless, he obliges when I ask if he'll come with me to Bernie's to buy a few tickets. Still, Joe isn't one to squander his luck. We agree that he'll pick six sets of numbers and we'll each play them—"so we share it in case the numbers hit."

Bernie's is just like any other corner store except for three big blowups of winning lottery checks, totaling $2,653,562.50, hanging behind the counter, all signed to Joseph J. Hornick, Sr. As a woman ran the cards, I asked Joe if he expected to take another jackpot someday. "I hope I do," he answered. "I feel that I will once more before I croak." He paused. "And this time, I'll stuff the money in my pocket and run away before anybody hears about it."

I left wondering if Joe's winnings are a blessing or a curse. When I got home, I logged on to Pennsylvania's lottery website and checked our numbers—nothing. I was disappointed. But then I considered what it might be like to be Joe—an object of such weird envy, scorn, and improbable hope—and whether it's not luckier to lose.

The Saint of Sin City

Charlie Bolin was backstage at Splash, a topless revue at the Riviera Hotel and Casino in Las Vegas, talking to a stagehand. When he held out his business card for the man, a dancer from the show, wrapped in a towel, approached Bolin and asked if she could have a card, too. He handed her one. She then looked him in the eye, opened her towel, and, breasts exposed, said coyly, "Oh, gee, I have nowhere to put it."

Bolin was unfazed. "I can see that," he deadpanned. "Tell you what. When you're dressed, drop by my Bible study, and I'll give you a card then."

There's little that Bolin, the Riviera's fifty-five-year-old chaplain, hasn't seen since he first preached on the Vegas strip more than thirty years ago. Showgirls and exotic dancers, card dealers and cocktail waitresses, gamblers and prostitutes, and victims of all manner of self-destruction, addiction, and abuse have come to him for counseling. He's prayed with Johnny Cash, Glen Campbell, Marilyn McCoo, and Natalie Cole. When one of the Flying Elvi, those daredevils who jump from planes dressed like the King, misjudged his landing and crashed "face-first" into a parked car, sustaining massive head injuries, Bolin was summoned to the scene to console the impersonator's sideburned brethren. (Exceeding the doctors' expectations, the stunt-man survived. "And he's back jumping today," Bolin said.)

Charlie Chaplain, as Bolin is fondly known, is the only full-time clergyman on a Vegas casino's payroll. For years, Bolin, an ordained Southern Baptist minister, volunteered his time up and down the strip, offering backstage Bible studies to cast and crew members yearning for a dose of eternal truth between shows. Since the Riviera took him on in 1993, he's on twenty-four-hour call to tend to the spiritual needs of the hotel's two thousand employees and more than four thousand daily guests.

Those needs can be significant. "Las Vegas is a tough place to work and play," Bolin says. "Studies show that simply being in a casino, whether as an employee or a guest, is very stressful. All those lights and sounds are designed to stimulate you and can be overwhelming. You may not even be aware of it, but being in a casino is like standing next to a buzz saw all day. It'll drive you crazy!"

So will living on the strip. Not a day goes by without a crisis for Bolin to handle. "It may be someone who's dealing with an addiction or a terminal illness," he says. "Or it may be a suicide or a guest who's died and their spouse needs to make arrangements. With employees, it's usually relationship problems. In many couples, both partners work, often at night and in different shifts, 24/7, which is particularly tough if they have kids. I know couples who only see each other three hours a week, max."

Bolin considers his position at the Riviera a "dream job" that took him twenty-six years to land. In 1967, when he was a sophomore at California Baptist College in Riverside, he drove to a small church in Las Vegas to preach at a revival. He became good friends with the church's pastor, who ran a street ministry on the Vegas strip, and Bolin returned once a month to help. He enjoyed working directly with the homeless, the poor, and the needy, and he briefly considered entering social work. In 1970, the year Bolin graduated college, the pastor in Vegas suggested he attend Golden Gate Baptist Theological Seminary in northern California and become his associate. "So I did," Bolin says. "I went to seminary specifically to become a chaplain on the Vegas strip."

After seminary, however, Bolin got "sidetracked." For the next nine years he ran a plumbing business in California. "But I wasn't happy," he said. "Finally, in 1982, I felt called to return to Vegas, to help my friend with his work on the streets. So I gave up my business and moved." For the next eleven years, Bolin ran backstage Bible studies and performed weddings to support himself.

In 1993, Jerry Grippe, the Riviera's vice president of operations, recognized Bolin's people skills and offered him a full-time gig. Bolin likens his position to that of a military chaplain, a role he filled in the Air Force Reserve. Grippe is a retired Army colonel. "He understands the value of having a chaplain around to keep the troops going," says Bolin. "The Riviera is a corporation, and corporations have trouble relating to employees as people. That's where I come in, providing pastoral and human services." The only thing Bolin's official duties don't include is weddings. (Though he will perform them, as well as funerals, on the side.)

Bolin downplays the exotic milieu in which he works— "being a chaplain in a casino is no different than being a chaplain in any city," he says—and he takes exception to Las Vegas's reputation as the American Sodom and Gomorrah. "Give me a break!" he says. "Go to Los Angeles, go to Chicago, go to New York. Those places are bad. I've been to North Beach in San Francisco—what a hole! And they call us Sin City?"

When pressed, Bolin concedes that Las Vegas is, okay, a bit surreal. "Sure. It's a fantasy world. Where else can you get a free hotel room? Where else can you get a prime-rib dinner for five bucks? And as with any fantasy, people are drawn to Vegas to escape their problems. Thing is, their problems don't go away once they're here, and if they get caught up in that fantasy, it can destroy them."

Not to mention that the offertory plates passed around at his Sunday services at the hotel often come back stacked with chips—"we just take 'em down and cash 'em in." (The proceeds support his volunteer staff.) Or the stripper who asked him to watch her act, in which she danced to "Operator (Get Me Jesus on the Line)," because she was afraid it was sacrilegious. Or that each Easter he gets some disappointed customers for his highly popular Passion play, which Bolin puckishly advertises next to the sign for a show featuring half-naked women. There's always a few who think, says Bolin, "Ah, Passion play, more sex!"

Occasionally, he has competition. One reformed topless dancer returned to a strip club to save her former cohorts. "She'd stand backstage and tell the girls they were going to hell," Bolin says. "She got kicked out. When they tried to kick me out, the girls defended me, saying, 'Oh, no. We want Charlie here because we can talk to him.'"

His popularity rests precisely on his refusal to judge. Bolin, who wears a collar, prefers to "allow people to be directed by God rather than me." He doesn't speak out against drinking, gambling, or topless dancing. This may come as no surprise, considering his employer. "I get criticism from Christians who say, 'Why aren't you telling people they shouldn't be in casinos?'" he says. "I've got a good answer for that. There are no job openings in the Trinity, I reply, including the job of Holy Spirit. It's not my place to tell people what is and is not a sin. I'm here to help people sort out what's going on in their spiritual lives and to help them hear what the Holy Spirit is telling them.

"My ministry is much like Jesus' ministering in the marketplace," he says. "Jesus frequently hung out with prostitutes and publicans, dishonest businessmen. And that's what he was criticized for! And today, a lot of conservative Christians choose to ignore that fact.

"I know the Holy Spirit is with me," he adds. "When I'm making my rounds on the floor, checking in on dealers, bartenders, and waitresses, they'll say, 'Boy, I feel much better when you're here.' I don't need to say much. Sometimes, I say nothing. They know who I am, and they know what I believe."

Among the Christian Booksellers

Though I am not an evangelical, I would not have missed the Christian Booksellers Association convention in Denver for the world. What was I doing there? Perhaps I'd better begin with a confession: I am a book convention junkie.

There are thousands of us junkies in this country, and if you've ever been to meetings of the American Booksellers Association, the American Library Association, or the American Academy of Religion, you've surely seen us. We're the feverish, wide-eyed folk who drift glacierlike through the exhibit aisles in search of promotional freebies. Our weakness is free books, posters, buttons, pens, publishers' customized bags, and food. We live for brief encounters with famous (and not-so-famous) authors and count it a personal failure when we can't wangle an invitation to an important party. I attended my first book show in 1991, and I've been hooked ever since.

This was my second CBA, and, I must say, it is fast becoming my favorite convention. Not only does it offer an unparalleled array of bumper stickers, pins, refrigerator magnets, pencils, greeting cards, and T-shirts, each embossed with a religious message, but it also provides "ample opportunities for spiritual refreshment," which that year included worship services, concerts, and special events featuring such heavies as Chuck Colson, Pat Robertson, and James Dobson, as well as the next tier of evangelical celebrities, such as Josh McDowell, Chuck Bolte, Jack Hayford, Larnelle Harris, Susan Ashton, Michael W. Smith, and Carman.

Each CBA has a theme, and that year it was "higher ground." "Whether you're a rookie sales associate or a seasoned owner/manager," an association brochure explained, "the CBA convention can help you soar as a professional bookseller." "Guaranteed to take your breath away," the brochure continued, the convention boasted more than 300,000 square feet of exhibitors' booths and some forty educational sessions designed to help Christian retailers make their stores the best they can be—"not in the name of the bottom line, but in the name of Jesus Christ." The accumulated effect was a "power-packed six days aimed at taking you up to some seriously higher ground." And you can't find much higher ground than Denver. At nearly five thousand feet, I had two nosebleeds my first day there.

Actually, Denver is the perfect venue for the CBA. Sure, it has its share of crime and racial problems, but downtown Denver is as family-oriented and all-American as a city can hope to be. The shopkeepers sweep the streets (I witnessed this twice), the men sport cowboy boots and hats, and families stroll the streets holding hands. Denver even has a baseball stadium named after a beer (Coors Field), and there's a Hooters restaurant on the Sixteenth Street Mall (which for some reason wasn't listed in the CBA convention guide). The general atmosphere of hospitality was so catching that I found myself smiling and nodding inanely at total strangers.

But I had little time to linger downtown. My schedule was packed with CBA events, the first of which was the Evangelical Christian Publishers Association's annual banquet and Gold Medallion Book Awards ceremony. The dinner drew hundreds of publishers, retailers, and their families, and was actually lots of fun—particularly after a few drinks. You have to grab an alcoholic drink elsewhere, however; the only drink served was a lime Kool-Aid concoction we called bug juice at summer Bible camp.

I was seated with a group of Christian publishers who regaled me with tales of their recent attempts to infiltrate China and Russia with Bibles. They spoke of visiting palaces and dignitaries. One executive had even met with Mikhail Gorbachev. The conversation flowed nicely, and our spirits were high, until the food arrived—small portions of chicken royale and asparagus spears. I was pleased, but everyone else at my table stared at their plates in disbelief. Somebody finally broke the spell by suggesting Burger King afterward. How these finicky folk coped with all those bland fish dinners they serve in Russia intrigued me, so I asked them about it. "The McDonald's in Moscow," one of them finally confessed.

For me, the big disappointment of the evening was that the keynote speaker, Elizabeth Dole, did not show up, because, the announcer said, of a blocked artery. I'd been looking forward to the address, hoping she might shed some light on why she and Bob had suddenly stopped attending the Methodist church in Washington, D.C., where the Clintons often worshiped. It was strange that none of the many prayers, blessings, and supplications issued that night mentioned Elizabeth Dole's health. I guess the question on everybody's mind was "Who will speak in Dole's place?" Ralph Reed? Pat Buchanan?

Instead, we listened to bestselling author Max Lucado, who was, for my money, the most thoughtful and engaging speaker at the entire convention. Handsome in a way that TV news broadcasters and real-estate agents often are, Lucado has all the charm of a true storyteller and the voice of a Southern preacher, which makes perfect sense because, as pulpit minister of the Oak Hills Church of Christ in Texas, that's exactly what he is.

Lucado gave a call to unity among Christians across denominational and traditional lines. He likened Christians to sailors on the same boat with "one captain, one destination," despite their different responsibilities and ideas about how to communicate with one another and the captain. "Sometimes the boat can be an unsafe place," he said. "Fights have broken out between sailors. And there are certain sailors on this boat who deny the existence of other sailors on this boat."

Adroitly switching metaphors, Lucado said that, for Jesus, "the fruit is more important than the name of the orchard." He urged acceptance between Protestants and Catholics, Baptists and Presbyterians. This was a powerful message— and controversial, considering that many CBA sailor-farmers have defined themselves largely by sucker punching other sailor-farmers within the association.

Then—dim the lights, cue the drumroll—the highlight of the evening: the Gold Medallion Book Awards to honor publishers of Christian books in twenty-two categories. The ceremony curiously lacked the sophisticated elegance you might expect at such an occasion. Spotlights swept the audience, a prerecorded announcer's voice reverberated off the walls, and images of the jacket covers flashed on huge screens at either end of the auditorium. The music wasn't exactly my taste—seventies-style Muzak with lots of drums and trumpets in classical mixes and bouncy polka numbers—but still, all the pomp and drama stirred in me an almost Proustian longing for the sights and sounds of an early childhood experience I had all but forgotten—the Amway pageants my mother used to drag me to.

Book award nominees included *Coming out of Homosexuality,* by Bob Davies and Lori Rentzel, *Lord, I Haven't Talked to You Since the Last Crisis, But . . .* , by Lorraine Peterson, and *Worms in My Tea: And Other Mixed Blessings,* by Becky Freeman and Ruthie Arnold. I later learned that Lucado's *When God Whispers Your Name* won the Gold Medallion Christian Book of the Year Award. Well before that award was announced I decided to sneak back to my hotel for a nightcap—or two.

Sunday morning I hauled myself out of bed to make the CBA worship service at the convention center. It was definitely worth the effort. The sermon was delivered by Tony Evans, cofounder and senior pastor of the three-thousand-member Oak Cliff Bible Fellowship in Dallas. He is also the chaplain of the Dallas Mavericks, a position he once held with the Dallas Cowboys—and it's easy to see why: Only a big, strapping, booming man like Evans could command the respect and attention of a professional sports team. If he ever decided to give up the ministry, I'm sure he could carve a brilliant career for himself as a prison guard.

Evans's impassioned sermon was on misguided love—"Do we really love God the way God wants us to love him? Do we adore his son the way he deserves to be adored?" But when I reviewed my notes I realized that Evans's sermon was mostly about food. All of his illustrations (except for an account of the final fight scene in *Rocky V*) revolved around eating and drinking. There was fried chicken. (Once at an airport restaurant, just as his flight was called, Evans was served a steaming plate of fried chicken, which "put me in a terrible catch-22," he said. "Finally I decided to take the fried chicken with me on the plane. God doesn't want you to sacrifice. You can eat that chicken, just don't miss the plane!") There were lollipops. (To calm Evans's son before administering an asthma shot, the family doctor gave the boy some candy: "Jesus is our lollipop!") Lemonade. ("The good news about God is he can take the lemons and make lemonade, take our sour decisions of the past and make them sweet.") Cooking. ("Ladies, when you married, you cooked for your husbands because you loved them. Now you cook just 'cuz you gotta eat, too! You've lost your first love.") And tea. ("How many of you are tea drinkers? There are two ways to make tea—dip or steep. We've got a lot of dippin' Christians today. Dip in Sunday, dip out!") I found something terribly unsettling about the sermon—probably the fact that he delivered it so close to lunch.

After a quick bite to eat I had another nosebleed, so I went back to my hotel to rest and read my free copy of *Tony Evans Speaks Out on Gambling and the Lottery*, which Moody Press offered all of us as we left the worship service (my first CBA souvenir!).

Monday morning marked the moment I'd been waiting for, the official opening of the convention floor. I dressed quickly and raced to the convention center. Hundreds of people were huddled outside, like the crowds that block the sidewalks the first morning of Macy's after-Christmas sale. Then, as if someone had fired a starting gun, the doors were flung open and we rushed in.

What lay before me was a convention junkie's heaven: aisle after aisle of more than 350 booths featuring books, music, and "holy hardware"—the religious napkin holders, sweatshirts, placards, and figurines that Christian retailers are famous for. Books account for just 28 percent of the CBA's $3-billion-a-year retail market, so it's fitting that a task force met during the convention to discuss the possibility of dropping the word *book* from the association's name. (A cynical friend suggested they rename it the Christian Trinket Association.)

It's odd that a market so heavily driven by nonbook products has an awards ceremony for books but not for the "sideline" merchandise that is its financial bread and butter. To rectify this lacuna, I decided to give out my own awards.

Best retail booth: Every year the major contemporary Christian music companies such as Word, Benson, and Alliance have the largest and, I imagine, most expensive booths at CBA. These are towering structures with private listening stations, state-of-the-art sound systems, and large screens that constantly play Christian music videos, which are essentially imitations of MTV videos only less interesting because the dancing is bad (Amy Grant must wear diving boots) and all the songs basically spin the same simple message about sin and salvation.

My award went to a T-shirt company called Living Epistles, which put itself on the map with its "Lord's Gym" sweat-shirt—a play on the "Gold's Gym" shirt Arnold Schwarze-negger made famous back in his *Pumping Iron* days. In the Living Epistles's version, the pumped-up, steroid-loaded bodybuilder is Jesus, and he's pressing himself up on a pile of rocks, blood gushing from his crown of thorns, and the enormous cross on his back reads, "The Sin of the World." The caption says, "Bench Press This!" On the other side is Jesus' palm pierced with a railroad spike and covered in blood. Inscribed are the words "His Pain, Your Gain."

Living Epistles has sold more than a million of these shirts, and at CBA the company commemorated its success with an enormous display—a fourteen-foot-tall statue of the "Lord's Gym" Jesus figure "bench-pressing" the Sin of the World. The stucco structure weighed fifteen hundred pounds and sat atop a base resembling a wall of lockers.

Best T-shirt: There are so many shirts at CBA that you could open a T-shirt-only shopping mall with them. No less startling than the number of these shirts are the slogans they carry, such as "Salvation Is Not for Wimps," "Jesus Loved You So Much It Hurt!" "Can a Moral Wrong Be a Civil Right?" "High Flyin', Death Defyin', Devil Dunkin', Power Jam for the Spiri-tual 'Stuff': Air Jesus," "His Blood's for You," and "God's Last Name is NOT Dammit." But the award goes to "God Made Grandmas So Kids Could Feel His Hugs."

Best bumper sticker: "Real Men Love Jesus."

Best trinket: Despite stiff competition from a bag of Scripture fortune cookies and a camouflage pen that reads, "Jesus Wants You to Be All You Can Be," the award goes to a soccer-ball key chain inscribed with "Jesus Is My Goal."

Best Christian children's board game: "The Game of Pilgrim's Progress." Based on Bunyan's book, this game enables us to relive Christian's journey by advancing board pieces from the City of Destruction to the Celestial City. An "excellent teaching and devotional tool" and "rich in spiritual applications," it features "custom pilgrims with detachable burdens."

Best poster: An F-15 fighter jet in vertical flight, below which is written Isaiah 40:31: "They shall mount up with wings of eagles."

Best surprise celebrity appearance: Remember Willie Aames? Years ago he played Tommy Bradford on *Eight Is Enough.* Today, Aames dresses in a purple superhero cape and plays Bibleman in a musical video series about a bunch of twelve-year-olds who put on skits about the Bible in their garage. Dressed in his Bibleman outfit, Aames was at the booth of the video company, Sparrow, posing for Polaroids with children. I waited in line twenty minutes before giving up.

Best scandal of the year: No convention is complete without a good scandal, and that year's CBA did not disappoint. But poor Oxford University Press. Or rather, poor Hargis

Thomas, Oxford's sales director. I've known Hargis for years and can vouch that he's the nicest guy you could ever meet. True, I've heard he occasionally fudges the score at the annual Oxford-Guideposts CBA softball game, but that in no way excuses what happened to him.

On Friday night convention workers were supposed to install Oxford University Press's light-box displays touting its lead fall Bible titles. When Hargis and his crew arrived at the booth Saturday morning, they stared in shock at their displays. Instead of transparencies for their new Scofield Special Editions and the Holy Bible with Illustrations from the Vatican Library, they found posters mounted for two Oxford titles they did not bring to the CBA—*Fetish*, which pictured a dominatrix dressed in full-leather gear ("cinched tight," Hargis explained, "in all the right places"), and *With Pleasure*, which showed a woman seductively biting a man's ear. Hargis also found snickerings and bemused notes left by other exhibitors.

I still can't figure out why he brought these salacious posters with him to Denver, and nobody knew why the convention workers mounted them in his booth. And that was the second time such a mistake was made! The year before, they mounted *The Oxford Companion to Wine* and *The Monkey Wars*, a book advocating the rights of animals in scientific experiments, in place of *The Precise Parallel New Testament* and another Scofield edition. Coincidence or conspiracy? You be the judge.

Hallowed Be Thy ... Whatsyourname

In the SUV waiting at the corner, the British news team was ticked. The crew from ITV had been having trouble all day tracking the holy man known as Whatsyourname, and now they were anxious about getting him to a studio in Philadelphia, a hundred miles away, in time for a live satellite interview. Whatsyourname had refused to ride with them. "I'd like, in fact, I insist, that John drive me," he told them. In the car he told me, "I don't like their attitude."

Then, as we were about to drive off, two priests ran up, waving and tapping frantically at my car window. They were from Poland, they explained. They were passing by when they recognized my passenger walking along the icy sidewalk in his bare feet and white robe. "We saw you on television and just had to tell you what an inspiration your ministry is!"

After ten minutes of this, the SUV backed up. The cameraman glowered at us from behind the wheel.

Whatsyourname, as he likes to be called, is an itinerant preacher who, from the robe to the beard and shoulder-length hair, is a dead ringer for Jesus. More precisely, he bears an uncanny resemblance to Warner Sallman's popular 1941 portrait, *Head of Christ*, which was reproduced 500 million times, becoming one of the most recognizable images of the twentieth century. Whatsyourname strolled into Hazleton, Pennsylvania, seemingly out of nowhere, in October 1999. He preached on the streets and when asked his name would reply, "What's your name?" Even after the local paper revealed him to be Carl J. Joseph, 39, Whatsyourname stuck.

People knew only what little he had revealed—that he'd taken a vow of poverty and lived on charity; that he claimed he was called to spread the gospel, a mission he started nine years ago. He said his mission had already taken him through forty-seven states and thirteen countries. Police ran a check and found nothing of concern—an arrest in Ohio for failing to disband a disorderly crowd gathered to hear him preach. (Charges were dismissed.) The Reverend Gerard Angelo, pastor of the Shrine of the Sacred Heart of Jesus, visited Whatsyourname and deemed him genuine. "He has a strong religious faith and doesn't claim to be Jesus." Eventually, Father Angelo invited the missionary to participate in a mass.

Soon Whatsyourname had ignited a revival in the predominantly Catholic area. When he appeared on *The Sam Lesante Show*, a favorite local program, the show got so many calls they had him back three times in two months. Nursing homes and hospitals beckoned. Thousands flocked to hear him speak at local churches. "People who haven't been to church in thirty years are returning," said Angelo. "I've never seen anything like it." Miracle stories abound—including one about a car suddenly repaired after Whatsyourname placed his hands on the hood. *Time* magazine and *20/20* came calling.

In *Training in Christianity*, the philosopher Søren Kierkegaard pondered what it would be like to be a follower in the presence of Jesus. He wrote that nineteenth-century Christians vainly believed that if they'd been around at the time of Christ, they would have instantly recognized him as the Son of God and rallied behind him. Kierkegaard disagreed: Jesus looked so much like every other Joe that his divinity was utterly unrecognizable. That's why his claims to be God were considered an offense to reason and demanded a leap of faith. Kierkegaard said his fellow Christians, failing to find an idealized Christ, would have responded to Jesus as others did—by crucifying him.

After Whatsyourname addressed a senior religion class at Hazleton's Bishop Hafey High School, the principal told the local paper, "He confronts you with the question, What if Jesus was here?" But how so? Jesus' own appearance caused people not to believe in him. Yet Whatsyourname, who resembles a popular twentieth-century image of Jesus, somehow inspires an amazing, spontaneous display of faith in Christ without seeming to challenge anyone's reason. Kierkegaard must be rolling over in his grave. This isn't faith, he'd say. It's idolatry.

The morning I arrived in Hazleton, I took a walk near the church where I was supposed to meet Whatsyourname. Along Broad Street, Hazleton's main drag, storefront after storefront is either empty or boarded up, giving the impression of a town badly in need of a miracle. Whatsyourname never showed, but before I had waited too long, Connie Muir, a local woman who assists Whatsyourname, came to take me to Sam Lesante's television studio. On the way, I asked about the day she first saw him.

"I was driving home from work," said Muir, "when I spotted this man in a white robe walking along the highway. Because it was October 25, I thought the robe was a Halloween costume.

Then I saw the bare feet, and I knew he was a missionary or prophet." She asked her son-in-law, who shares a small duplex with Connie's daughter, their two kids, and Connie's other two children, to drive back and offer the man a ride. "When my son-in-law brought him home, Whatsyourname walked in and said, 'Peace be with this house.'" He's lived there ever since, on a futon in the living room.

At Lesante's studio, the sight of Whatsyourname standing amid a blur of shirts and ties was surreal. Sam showed us to a conference room. "So, how are you?" Whatsyourname asked, his soft voice barely audible.

"Great," I said, and commented on the weather.

"But how is your spiritual life?"

"Oh. It's . . . a journey."

"Are you close to God?" His wide eyes peered into mine.

"My journey has its ups and downs," I said. "Some open highway, and, um, lots of toll booths." If there's anything I loathe, it's being expected to have pat answers for questions humankind has struggled with since the Garden of Eden.

"What do you make of the mystery of Christ?"

I slipped a tape into my recorder and rewound it. "Okay, then! What do you think draws people to you?"

Whatsyourname closed his eyes, took a deep breath, and tilted his head toward the ceiling.

"They come," he whispered, "they come because theirs is a search for answers. And I tell them to love one another. To reach within. To share that love with the One. And to share that love with all who choose to respond to it." Then he lowered his head, opened his eyes, and gazed at me, as if to say, *Next question.*

That evening, Whatsyourname and I attended mass at St. Joseph's. Every head followed Whatsyourname as he paced the center aisle, eyes fixed ahead, to a front pew. He's probably the closest thing to a celebrity this town has had in a long time, and he fills the role well. After the service, Whatsyourname sat quietly, meditating, I supposed. A frail woman in her eighties approached him meekly. Her husband was at home, gravely ill. Could Whatsyourname please, please visit him?

Waiting for Whatsyourname in the foyer were at least forty more people. A woman rushed over and clasped his hands. As he spoke with her, the others quietly formed a line behind her that ran the length of the room and snaked back. A drill everyone knew? One woman cried. Another hugged him. I saw him pray with at least six people. Whatsyourname stayed forty-five minutes, until he'd given each person an audience.

Back in the car, Whatsyourname seemed upbeat, more at ease than he had been earlier, as if ministering to these people had revitalized his spirit after a long day at the office, so to speak. Or maybe he was simply basking in the adoration of so many folks eager to touch the hem of his garment.

I asked what they discussed with him. "One guy had a legal problem," he said. "Another struggles with alcoholism, and I prayed with him. One woman asked whether it was okay to get divorced."

"What did you tell her?"

"That a true marriage is based on consent," he said. "God cares about our intent and not what we say in public. That was an insight to her."

Time magazine has noted the "whiff of disingenuousness [that] clings to" Whatsyourname. He refuses to discuss his own family, birthplace, or even where his many stories occurred, which invites you to imagine all sorts of outrageous—or perhaps utterly mundane—details he's afraid you'll discover. (*The Toledo Blade* has reported that, in 1991, Joseph was arrested for sneaking into an adult movie theater in that city. He pleaded no contest, the paper says, but later failed to appear for a court date.)

Whatsyourname does refer to a conversion experience spurred by a low point in "the mystery of evil." Kent Jackson, a reporter at the Hazleton *Standard-Speaker,* speculates that Whatsyourname's conversion is so complete that his past may be irrelevant and would only be a distraction to his ministry. Saints Paul and Matthew, of course, revealed their low points, as do evangelical preachers.

But who can question Whatsyourname's commitment, even if we're not sure what that is? I've watched him stand barefoot on a freezing night, talking for five minutes with a goofy teenager who, from what I could tell, merely wanted to see how long he could make Whatsyourname stand in the snow. And if Whatsyourname routinely sits all night with sick and dying strangers, as Connie Muir says he does, then perhaps he deserves the sainthood she believes is his destiny.

Still, it's the Jesus look I can't get past. When I asked about the robe, he said it was because he didn't want to support exploitative clothes manufacturers. "And I found that a loose-fitting garment is practical for living outdoors." Practical? In the snow? Admit it, I said, the getup is a huge reason you draw crowds (and, I didn't say, British television). "Of course," he said. "And the crowds hear the message."

I asked if there was ever a time he did all the same stuff—
walk town to town, preaching and praying with the sick—
but wore everyday clothes, like jeans and a T-shirt.

"Oh, sure," he said.

"How was that different?" I asked.

"Nobody paid attention."

The Video Messiah

While TV shopping for abs rollers, psychic phone pals, baldness cures, and diets guaranteed to make me lose thirty pounds in thirty days, I've sometimes asked myself when televangelists were going to break into infomercials. They have the talent for it, they have outlets, and they are not coy about asking for money.

My question got an answer one summer from none other than the Reverend Jerry Falwell, when I discovered him on cable delivering what at first appeared to be a fire-and-brimstone sermon on heeding God's call. "Let the truths of God's word," he urged, "the truths that have guided kings and princes and presidents and shoeshine boys for centuries, invade your life!" But when he started reciting lines like "act now" and "just four easy payments, all major credit cards accepted," I began to realize that this was not Falwell's standard Sunday broadcast from the Thomas Road Baptist Church in Lynchburg, Virginia.

No: It was a half-hour pitch for Falwell's "brand new and revolutionary" Institute of Biblical Studies—"the finest biblical studies program ever developed." The institute, I learned, is a six-videocassette study series that, "in just twelve hours of anointed teaching," explains everything you will ever need to know about the Bible "from Genesis to Revelation." "This new program"—Falwell beamed—"actually allows you to go to Bible college right in your own home." Why is it so special? "Because twenty-five years ago I founded Liberty University, and I can assure you this program was developed from the exact same material used in the world-famous introductory courses here at Liberty. That's how good the Institute of Biblical Studies is!"

An infomercial is effective if it argues compellingly that a product is: (a) essential; (b) easy to use; and (c) affordable. By these standards, Falwell's pitch rated an A plus. First, necessity: "The institute teaches you wisdom; it teaches you character traits that can actually help you succeed in business or at home. I'm telling you from my heart, if you are going to do just one thing this year, take one step to improve yourself, I urge you to take advantage of this special introductory offer."

Next, simplicity: "I want to make it abundantly clear that we have absolutely gone out of our way to make this simple enough, and easy enough, so that anyone can complete it, regardless of age, educational background, or any other factor."

Finally, cost: "If you went to Bible college, not only would you have to commute back and forth to school, but you would probably pay well over $1,000 in tuition costs alone. [The Institute of Bible Studies] is only $295—that's less than a dollar a day for a year of study!"

Curious about a program that, in lieu of divinity school, could have spared me a mountain of student loans, I bit. Because I ordered right away, I received a special hundred-dollar "scholarship," plus an extra discount for paying the whole cost at once, via my credit card. The package arrived promptly: six videos and a sixty-two-page study guide, which included not only "helpful charts and maps" but the final exam I had to complete and return to earn a diploma. Even more helpfully, the guide also provided an answer key for the exam.

Three tapes each are given to the Old and New Testaments; the instructor is Dr. Ed Hindson, described by Falwell as "one of the greatest Bible teachers to ever teach the word of God." Popping the first tape into my VCR, I was greeted by Dr. Hindson, a clean-cut, fortyish guy wearing a dark suit, bright red tie, and aviator glasses. Dr. Hindson outlined our mission: "When we sort out the difference between Abraham and Jacob, when we can tell the difference between a Hittite and a parasite, when we can tell the difference between Damascus and Babylon, all of a sudden you'll begin to realize these are real people, these are real places."

In the first lesson one learns that the world of Genesis was "a very different world than the world in which we live today." In those days, "people lived to be nine hundred years old" because there was a "vapor canopy" that enveloped the earth and "filtered out the infrared and ultraviolet rays and kept people from developing cancer and prevented fermentation from taking place." It was "a world in which dinosaurs could have survived" and "people could have grown to an enormous size. And yet all that changed with the flood."

In later tapes I was told the deeper meaning of the Exodus story about how the Israelites painted their door posts with blood to prepare for their escape from Egypt. "They began, without even knowing it, to make the sign of the cross—the indication of the redemption through the blood atonement of Jesus Christ that shall ultimately come." I was given an answer to the liberal scholars who suggest that the Red Sea through which Moses led his people was only a knee-deep swamp: "You don't drown [Pharaoh's soldiers] in water that's knee-deep!" The Book of Esther was neatly summarized: "the story of how the Jews are spared by a young girl who wins a beauty contest."

The New Testament tapes offered similar insights into the people of Jesus' day. The Gnostics were "kind of like New Agers before there was the New Age." The Herodians were extremists, the Pharisees were compromisers, and the Sadducees were liberals: "They were 'sad, you see,' because they didn't believe in the power of God."

It's on the tape—honest.

A notable difference in the tapes on the New Testament was the larger quota of sermonizing. Speaking of Jesus, Dr. Hindson says, "You can study all about him and know all the details of his life, but until you know, in your own heart and soul and life, him personally—as your own lord and savior—it's just so much information. And I'd like to urge you, right now, before you go one step further, to take a moment to acknowledge your sinfulness, your need of a savior, your need of salvation, and give your life to the Lord Jesus Christ, who will come in the power of his spirit and indwell you with the glory and the power and the life of God himself." I have to acknowledge, in my sinfulness, that too many lengthy passages in this vein reminded me of the power of the fast-forward control.

The best parts of the program were the Q & A periods—"Tough Questions and Timely Answers," in which Falwell himself replies to questions in an auditorium filled with "Liberty's brightest students." He is as lively and engaging as ever, so that it is only from the students' stilted questions that you can tell these allegedly spontaneous sessions were completely staged.

Q: Were there dinosaurs on the ark?

A: I'm no scientist, but I believe that men and dinosaurs were here together. I don't know what caused the extinction of dinosaurs, but their remains are here and the fossils are evidence without question. So, I believe that there was a healthy pair of dinosaurs on the ark and that they took up as much space as they wanted.

Q: How old is the earth?

A: I flip on the TV sometimes and there's Carl Sagan talking about something that happened forty billion years ago. On another program there's some agnostic or atheist saying that this rock is four billion years old. And I cannot help but smile, because we have without a doubt a young earth. We have a record that the earth has been here six thousand years. . . . People forget that God created Adam a fully grown and mature man with age built in. So God could have very easily built in the strata and the carbon dating and the fossil evidence.

Q: Is capital punishment correct today?

A: The Old Testament is very clear: "An eye for an eye, a tooth for a tooth." But there are many who say that under the new covenant . . . there's no place for it because Christ died on the cross. But the fact is, his death on the cross is the greatest evidence that capital punishment is acceptable today. If ever there was a platform to cry out against capital punishment, our Lord had it on the cross.

"My dream, my vision," Falwell explained in the infomercial, "is to actually put this program—listen!—in the hands of fifty thousand families and individuals. And what I am going to do to achieve this vision is to give [the special offer] to the first fifty thousand people who pick up that phone."

At $159 each, that's a gross of some $8 million. It's an incredible deal.

The Valley of Humiliation

CHRISTIAN: *As it was difficult coming up, so (so far as I can see) it is dangerous going down.*

PRUDENCE: *Yes, so it is; for it is an hard matter for a man to go down into the Valley of Humiliation, as thou art now, and to catch no slip by the way . . .*

So he began to go down, but very warily, yet he caught a slip or two.

I Was a Times Square
Street Preacher

On a miserably hot June afternoon in Times Square, passersby were weaving on the sidewalk to avoid a loud, caustic man who was making a show of himself. In a strident voice, he was crying out, telling everyone he saw that their souls were bound for hell. In a remote place in my brain, I was trying to figure out precisely what joy or purpose there is in intentionally annoying perfect strangers. I was particularly interested because I was that man—and that voice was mine.

"Excuse me, ma'am," I said to a middle-aged woman, a tourist probably, who'd stopped beneath the massive NBC screen on the Forty-third Street traffic island to mop her brow and remove her sweater. "If you think you're warm today, imagine how hot you'll feel when you're burning in hell!"

"What?" the woman said, looking up to see me clasping a large red Bible.

I offered her a pamphlet. "Here, maybe this will help you understand the dire condition of your soul."

She glanced at the tract briefly. "You've got to be kidding."

"No, ma'am," I replied. "Hell is no joke."

"Obnoxious," she muttered, and turned to walk away.

The woman was right, of course. Telling someone she is doomed to spend eternity choking on sulfur fumes and bobbing like a cork in the lake of fire is obnoxious. I've often had spiritual counsel screamed at me, and I sympathize with her completely.

But sympathize as I might, when it comes to street preaching, the meek definitely do not inherit the earth. As the woman stepped across Forty-third Street, I raised my Bible and shouted, "Obnoxious? Try telling that to God, sister, while your *toches* is getting flame-broiled at Satan's eternal tailgate party!"

Yes, reader, I was a street preacher. Well, for a day. Actually, I was a street preacher for three days, but I struggled with my nerve the first two. I mostly hung out at the WWF's new theme restaurant and bar on Broadway, watching taped wrestling matches and trying to assure myself that, in a world full of idiotic stunts, fake preaching is pretty harmless.

My experiment was intended to answer one question: Why would anybody want to be a street preacher? It's a very unpleasant job. The pay is lousy, the work potentially hazardous. Even dentists are better liked. I figured the act of street preaching must be fulfilling in itself. And there was one way to find out.

Where to preach was obvious. Times Square is a street preacher's paradise. Prophets and evangelists flock to the Crossroads of the World for the same reason corporate advertisers have claimed every inch of billboard space—it's all about eyeballs. At any one time, more people from more nations are milling around there than at any other spot on the planet.

A successful street preacher needs to have an eye-catching handout. One guy quietly distributed a simple red and white religious tract. After five minutes he had given away two, one to me, the other to a homeless lady. Now, the guy handing out cards for Legz Diamond's (also red and white) had more success, maybe one taker for every fifteen refusals, and he said far less to passersby. Of course, his handout depicted a woman's long, bare legs on one side and had the words "XXX All Nude Super Stars" inscribed on the other.

You also have to have a little bit of showbiz. A guy on Forty-sixth Street paced the sidewalk, reading flatly from an open Bible. Not a soul even paused. By contrast, a group who call themselves the Black Israelites were hands down the most spectacular street preaching I've witnessed, a tour de force. Four or five Black Israelites routinely and literally command the corner of Forty-fourth and Broadway, outside MTV. Wearing brightly colored satin robes covered with gold stars, they burn incense and have an entire table of tapes and literature, against which stands a sandwich board listing the Bill of Rights, which guarantees their freedom to be there. Two guys distribute flyers while another guy barks out the message at the top of his lungs.

Nonetheless, their message is a little hard to follow. Basically, white people are evil, and blacks are the only true descendants of the twelve tribes of Israel. But no matter: The look in one little old lady's eyes told me the Black Israelites had positively put the fear of God into her.

The next time out, I assembled my other props: a black folder in which to carry my tracts, and the Good Word—my big, red New Oxford Annotated Bible with the Apocrypha. I wished I had something less elitist, perhaps leather-bound and well thumbed. But it was the expanded scholar's edition, edited by Herbert G. May and Bruce M. Metzger. I thought it might give me extra authority if somebody knowledgeable started asking me questions and I got into a pinch.

The courage to preach came haltingly. The year before, I'd tried stand-up comedy on a lark, and I found telling jokes onstage for five minutes oddly less daunting than this. At least at the New York Comedy Club I was confident my routine wasn't too offensive, and I knew I had planted a friend in the audience who would laugh. In Times Square, I had no assurances.

At first, I just handed out my tracts. One person took a tract but didn't look at it. Another took one and threw it away right in front of me.

I started asking, "Excuse me, do you know the Truth?" I fared no better. So I tried, "Hey, you're going to hell!" as I whipped out a tract. This got more of a reaction, mostly annoyed and alarmed looks.

Then one guy told me, "Go fuck yourself." For some reason, he boosted my confidence. There wasn't much worse anyone could say, I realized. Or maybe I'd been out there long enough to be sure I wasn't going to get beat up. I developed a bounce in my step and felt almost giddy as I boldly told people they were damned. I was experiencing a street preacher's high, if you will—the freedom that comes with defying humiliation. Beyond that wall, there's the rush that self-righteousness gives.

Now, sickly, I selected my targets: I avoided anyone who exuded attitude or moved with purpose, preying instead on people who looked lost. A well-dressed businessman stepped out of the lunch-hour stampede along Broadway to make a cell-phone call. Before he finished dialing, he snapped the phone shut, sighed, and gazed skyward, a mixture of fatigue and frustration written across his face.

"Excuse me, sir," I said. "Did you know you're going to hell?"

He looked at me. "What?"

"According to Scripture," I said, hoisting my Oxford Annotated, "it's easier for a camel to pass through the eye of a needle than for a rich man to enter the kingdom of God." I paused, unable to read his expression. Uncertain, I added, "I'd say you look well off."

"Go to hell," he said, and walked away.

"Good for you, sir!" I shouted after him, and somewhere deep inside, I meant it.

Labor Pain

Here are the circumstances of my birth. My mother, who hadn't planned me and in fact was on the pill when I was conceived, didn't realize she was pregnant for four months. Her labor was excruciating, lasting sixty-three hours, and when the doctor tried to break her water, he found there was none. Only one in 3 million babies goes without amniotic fluid, but I beat the odds. This of course spelled trouble; it was feared, among other things, I would have no kidneys and would be severely deformed.

Next, I tried to come out sideways, but for some reason the obstetrician forwent a cesarean, electing instead to spend seven hours turning me before plucking me out with forceps. The last thing the doctor told my mother before she went under anesthesia was that she should "expect a monster."

Nevertheless, there I was in Sigalit's kitchen in the Mill Basin section of Brooklyn, and I didn't like what I was hearing. "What happens to people as they approach a rebirthing session usually reflects their actual birth experience," said Sigalit, my rebirthing therapist, as she served tea. We were waiting for the others in the group session to arrive. "For instance," Sigalit went on, "I just got a call from a woman down the street who's bringing her husband. He's still in bed and doesn't want to get up, which means as an infant he probably didn't want to leave the womb!"

I chuckled, but I wasn't terribly sympathetic. I had worked out my birthing experience—so I hoped—by parking the wrong way on a one-way street and getting a ticket, and I still managed to get there fifteen minutes early. "Others are probably delayed because of construction on the Belt Parkway," Sigalit said. "Maybe they got stuck in the birth canal."

An hour later, the latecomers and I were huddled in the basement. Sigalit put on a soft New Age tape, and we opened with meditation "to quiet ourselves and become fully present." Then we said our names, how we were feeling at that moment, and what we hoped to get out of the seminar. Of the twelve gathered, it turned out only five were students; the others were rebirthers (two students failed to show, stillbirths, presumably). Sigalit, I learned, is a drug and alcohol counselor who had come from Israel thirteen years ago. She got interested in rebirthing to overcome fears of giving birth herself.

Sigalit's coleader, Frederico Pina, now informed us that every thought and experience we have is "recorded in our cells." Unfortunately, as much as 97 percent of the sixty to seventy thousand thoughts we produce daily are negative. Most we repress to get by. "Negative thoughts are like drops of black ink added to a vase of water," Frederico said. "Each drop makes the water darker and darker. Breathing clears the ink out, like adding a cup of fresh water."

Rebirthing therapy, it turns out, is only incidentally about reentry into the world. The real point of the exercise is breathing, a lot of it, to flush out our repressed traumas—and the number-one trauma is birth. "At birth, we go from this warm, safe place to being pushed into a cold, noisy, bright world," explained Frederico, "where a stranger in a face mask separates us from our mother, turns us upside down, and smacks us on the rear end. No wonder many of us develop an aversion to authority figures."

Frederico and Sigalit took this quite literally. They distributed a four-page, single-spaced list of personality traits that different birth types engender. Children born by cesarean may feel in adulthood they can't do things for themselves and have a "fear of/fascination with knives." Breech babies live with guilt and a fear of hurting people they love. Late-birth babies are inclined to be tardy grown-ups. An infant that had the cord wrapped around its neck may show a "tendency to sabotage self" and "hate anything around the neck." Infants placed in incubators may develop a "fascination with machines." "Ever wonder why drugs were so big in the sixties?" Frederico asked. "Because after World War II, hospitals started using anesthesia, so a whole generation grew up feeling they had to be numb when they underwent change."

For the group rebirth, Frederico showed us how to inhale and exhale deeply, without pause—"one continuous, circular breath." This we would do for an hour. "Don't worry if you have strange sensations," he said. "You may feel cold or start twitching. That's normal. And don't fight any thoughts or memories, however unpleasant. Release them, and remember you're in a safe place."

Not everyone is entirely safe. A ten-year-old girl in Denver died in 2000 during rebirthing therapy intended to help her bond with her adoptive mother. The girl, Candace New-maker, was wrapped in a blanket with both ends tied to sim-ulate the womb. She screamed more than fifty times that she couldn't breathe, but therapists pushed against her with pil-lows (labor contractions), urging her to struggle her way out to be "reborn." After the seventy-minute videotaped session, the blanket was unwrapped and Candace was found lying in vomit and excrement. She died of asphyxiation at a Denver hospital the next day. In 2001, the two unlicensed therapists began serving sixteen years each for reckless child abuse resulting in death, and Colorado has outlawed the technique.

Frederico and Sigalit assured us they were of the gentle, no-touching school, but I was still a little nervous, I guess. Sigalit had us arrange our blankets so all our heads extended toward the wall and our feet were in the middle of the room. "When we come to, we'll all be in an alien spacecraft trailing the Hale-Bopp comet," I murmured to the woman next to me. She looked perplexed. Then the lights went out.

Once we had the breathing rhythm down, the sound was otherworldly—eight or nine sets of lungs panting simulta-neously in the dark, like a moment out of *The Blair Witch Project* or a really perverse phone call. Huffing and puffing, I thought, How can I sustain this for an hour? What if I hyper-ventilate? More important, I found, was not to let myself focus on the silliness of the scene. I feared I'd burst out laughing.

Eventually, unexpectedly, my arms and legs began to tingle. Waves of energy swept over me. I felt great. The sound of the others' breathing gradually receded, and I felt light, like I could float up off the floor.

Vivid memories came flooding in. I was in Europe, reliving exhilarating moments from my backpacking trek across Spain a few years before. First, I was hiking the Pyrenees, taking long strides and gulping tons of fresh air. Then I was crossing the vast wheat fields of the *meseta,* not another soul for miles, just me and the wheat under a huge blue sky. A woman in the room started crying, but I didn't care. I was far away, having a ball. A cell phone rang, snapping me from my reverie. I ignored it and kept breathing.

Next I was in my high school friend's basement, getting stoned and laughing. A voice whispered, "Breathe, John, breathe. You're alive, you exist!" It was Sigalit, kneeling beside me. I'm fine, girl, I thought. Don't worry about me.

When Frederico's voice gently brought us back to earth and I opened my eyes, I felt refreshed. Frederico came over to me. "Did you feel like a monster?" he asked, a little expectantly. I was tempted to tell him I had been through hell there on the floor. I guess I had wanted more out of the experience. Luckily, when Sigalit came up to ask me how things had gone, I answered that it was actually quite pleasant. "I know," she said. How? "It's my job to know."

When I got home, I called my mother, who recalled my birth. "When I came to, I'd fully accepted that you'd be this torn-up freak of a thing," she said, "but you looked like a perfect angel." I thought about rebirthing myself into a wheat field in Spain and into a basement stoners' session. I had beaten the odds again.

Fast Forward

Day One

My hope is that if I don't obsess about the fact that I'm not eating, I won't dwell on how much I wish I were. Just focus on work, I tell myself. After all, Moses and Jesus didn't panic about their fasts, or at least the Bible doesn't mention it. And they went forty days. I'm planning only seven, and I'm allowing myself a glass of juice a day. I remind myself of the benefits practitioners claim I'll reap if I stick it out— enhanced health and creative energy, deeper rest and relaxation, greater spiritual awareness.

When a pang of hunger strikes midafternoon, I drink a quart of spring water. This seems to work, at least until just before bed, when I make the mistake of going into the kitchen to get a phone number. A feeling of comfort and relief sweeps over me. I realize it's because I'm where the food is. Here in my kitchen, no matter how tough the day's been, I can retreat and prepare myself a nice bowl of soup. Not tonight. Or tomorrow night, or the night after that. I'm getting panicky again. Then, as I leave the room, I glance at the sink and discover a benefit of fasting I hadn't considered: no dirty dishes to wash.

Day Two

Paul and Patricia Bragg's book, *The Miracle of Fasting*, points out that everything we ingest, even the air we breathe, is full of toxins that are poisoning us. This is pretty comforting right now. Fasting, the Braggs say, allows our digestive system, made up of our largest and most energy-consuming organs, to rest. The body can use that energy to rid itself of a lifetime's accumulation of metabolic crap. Today's the day to dwell on that crap.

But as you detox, there are ill effects, and I'm becoming acquainted with several of them—fatigue, dizziness, irritability, headaches. My tongue feels thick and pasty, and I have an unpleasant taste in my mouth. But, oddly, I swing from being sluggish one hour to feeling energetic and ready for a jog the next.

I go into New York to run some errands. Hot dog stands and falafel joints usually have no appeal for me, but today they beckon. I have to pause at a street corner until a wave of nausea and light-headedness passes.

I run into an acquaintance—a hip, young art dealer who once sold me some paintings and is eager to sell me some more. I explain that I'm fasting, with five days to go, and that I need to get some juice. "Let's grab a cocktail," he says, in utter seriousness. Clearly, he doesn't get the whole fasting thing, and I'm slightly embarrassed I mentioned it.

Jesus, of course, lets the devil take him to the top of the Temple, so I go with the art dealer to Balthazar, a trendy SoHo restaurant known for its "French comfort food." We make our way to the bar. I feel like Christian in *Pilgrim's Progress*, when he wanders into Vanity Fair. Only I've stumbled into the shrine of a food cult. I'm struck by how the stomach affects our perception of the material world. Balthazar is packed with the beautiful and the damned—models, artists, and investment bankers—lounging in deep red banquettes and consuming pâté en croûte, moules frites, duck shepherd's pie. I want it all, but the absurdity of it all also glares at me.

We sit down at the bar. Within my reach are a dish of ripe olives, a bowl of hard-boiled eggs, and a plate of flatbread— a holy man's repast, fast-breaking food. Marshaling all my resolve, I order spring water and a tomato juice. "Why not make it a Bloody Mary?" my dealer friend persists. "It's not like it's food, right?"

Day Three

I open a can of cat food and pause before I spoon it into the cats' bowls. I'd never noticed before how much the Science Diet feline maintenance formula resembles a juicy slab of meat loaf. I hold the can to my nose, close my eyes, and sniff. It even smells like meat loaf, sort of, with fish mixed in. Not bad. I examine the label: liver and chicken recipe—mmmm. Meat by-products, powdered cellulose, locust bean gum— ooooh!

Day Four

My skin feels tighter, my face has a glow. My muscles are taut, healthy, as if I've been exercising. Everything I see— buildings, people, the trash in the streets—continues to look sharper, brighter. At a bookstore, I get an intoxicating whiff of perfume. I look for its bearer. The only other customer in the store, a woman, is three aisles away.

But by the time I make my purchase, fatigue has returned. The paperback I bought weighs on my arm like luggage. When someone on the street drives his shoulder into me, intentionally, it seems, I'm too exhausted to get upset. No wonder Gandhi could maintain a cool head while liberating India from the British Empire. Fasting takes the piss and vinegar out of you.

Day Five

Late night at the office. The boss has ordered in Chinese for everyone. When the food arrives, my colleagues eat, talk, and laugh. I alone sit glued to my computer fifteen feet away. The air fills with the aromas of dishes, but I don't allow my brain to identify them by name. But to my surprise, these smells excite no hunger in me anyway.

Having learned my lesson earlier in the week, I've decided to follow Jesus' teaching that we should fast in secret. He meant that we shouldn't show off. But he probably also knew that if no one knows you're fasting, they're less likely to try to tempt you with Bloody Marys and Peking duck.

Day Six

The last day or two have been wonderful. I haven't been hungry at all, and my energy level, on the whole, has been high. I'm able to concentrate harder and think more clearly than usual. I am also able to relax more deeply, and I've slept more soundly than I can remember.

I enjoy not eating now, revel in my discipline. A guy across from me on the train home tears through a Big Mac and two bags of french fries as if his life depended on it. I

watch him shovel greasy fries into his mouth, where a frag-
ment of special sauce glistens on his lip. I am revolted. A
feeling of, admittedly, pharisaical superiority comes over
me. Compared to this guy, I am pure spiritual fire. Why do I
ever need to go back to solid food?

Day Seven

I feel terrific all morning. I'd resolved not to let vanity enter
into my fast, but I slip and weigh myself. I've lost twelve
pounds. I pay for my hubris in the afternoon as the worm
turns. I feel sick to my empty stomach. This might be
because, earlier, I crammed a whole head of garlic into my
juicer, ran it with just a couple of carrots, and drank the
result. My skin, especially on my face and head, is burning.
I'm dizzier now than I've been all week. This article is due,
but now I can't bring myself to sit down and write.

My dire state, I decide, may have nothing to do with the
garlic but be rather an illness brought on by fasting. Or has
my body unlocked a deeper, more sinister mother lode of
toxins somewhere? I lie down and sleep for three hours.

When I wake up, I find I'm reluctant to break my fast. The
worst of the seven days has been the havoc fasting has
wreaked on my social life. As it is, I've already skipped two
dinner parties, and I'm sure my coworkers, who love to rib
me about my fast, will still be making jokes about it months
after I'm back on solid food. But saying no to consumption,
to excess—the twin pillars of our culture—has given me a
sense of freedom and its own weird satisfaction. I've become
a little attached to nonattachment. Part of me wants to
extend the fast to a full month. And I know I can do it.

The Valley of the
Shadow of Death

CHRISTIAN: But what have you seen?

MEN: Seen! Why the Valley itself, which is as dark as pitch; we also saw there the hobgoblins, satyrs, and dragons of the pit: we heard also in that Valley a continual howling and yelling, as of people under unutterable misery who there sat bound in affliction and irons: . . . in a word, it is every whit dreadful, being utterly without order.

We See Dead People

In some ways, Echo Bodine and I were like the other couples visiting open houses that Sunday afternoon. We were neatly dressed, we had an itinerary (a carefully studied Minneapolis *Star Tribune* real-estate section), and we knew exactly what we were looking for. Unlike other couples, however, we weren't interested in location, price, or how well the pipes would hold up come winter. No, we were there to check out strange vibes, inexplicable sounds, white light, and clouds of energy—particularly clouds in a human shape.

In other words, we were looking for dead people—"just looking for ghosts," as Echo flatly told one real-estate agent who asked what he could help us find—spirits who, for various reasons, would rather bang around in an attic and scare the bejeezus out of the living than kick back in paradise with departed friends and loved ones.

Echo Bodine is a professional ghostbuster, or ghost counselor, as she also calls herself. A psychic and spiritual healer based in the Twin Cities, she talks to ghosts and often *argues* with them as she attempts to coax the more stubborn among them "down the tunnel and into the light."

Though she's been featured on shows such as *Sally Jessy Raphaël* and NBC's *The Other Side*, I discovered Echo through her latest book, *Relax, It's Only a Ghost: My Adventures with Spirits, Hauntings, and Things That Go Bump in the Night.* Echo's otherworldly encounters were so deliciously odd, I couldn't set the book down. There was Bill, a policeman ghost who protected the women who worked in a "massage parlor." When Echo confronted him, Bill confessed that he tore down a shower curtain out of anger when he realized one john was a priest.

On another ghostbusting, Echo met a female spirit who had such a crush on a guy (living) that, whenever he brought a woman home, the ghost would slap him silly and throw him against a wall. Best of all, the guy was six-foot-three and *enjoyed* being tossed around by a jealous wraith! To his landlady's dismay, he insisted that if Echo busted his ghost, he'd move. Ultimately, man and ghost remained united.

Wow, I thought, the dead are just as screwed up as the living.

Eager to meet some residents of the Beyond for myself, I called Echo and asked if she would take me ghost hunting. She graciously assented but regretted that she didn't have any jobs at the moment. I proposed we tour open houses. "Cool," she said, and then, after a pause, blurted, "The governor's mansion! I read that Jesse Ventura told a school tour there's a ghost in his kitchen!" I booked a flight to Minneapolis online as we spoke.

I met Echo at the curb outside the governor's residence on Summit Avenue in St. Paul, where she pulled up in a sporty Geo convertible with a "Mean People Suck" bumper sticker affixed to its rear. A tall, pretty blonde, the fifty-three-year-old has a personality to match her car—spunky and fun, not an ounce of pretension. "I feel lots of vibes here," Echo whispered as we entered the English Tudor Revival–style mansion. "I mean, *lots* of vibes!"

The first thing I learned about ghost hunting is that it's difficult to do when you're in a group of twenty-five, being hustled from room to room by a tour guide who seems to fear for her job, or worse, should any of her lambs stray. "It'll be tough to pinpoint a ghost in all this commotion," Echo told me, as we crossed the main foyer. Besides the stream of tours, gubernatorial staffers and other officials were bouncing between several meetings, including, we were told, the Brain, formerly known as the Body. (We didn't see him, but a press aide did verify later that one evening, when he was alone, the governor went to check on a crash in the mansion's kitchen and found dishes all over the floor.)

I gave Echo space to conduct her psychic snooping, which she performed remarkably inconspicuously. Quiet concentration, mostly. If you didn't know better, you'd think she was trying to make out a distant sound or recall a shopping list.

After the tour, we retreated to a restaurant to debrief. "Well," I demanded, as we dug into salads, "what's the verdict?"

"Oh, the place is haunted, all right," Echo said. "There was a ghost on the first floor, beyond the hallway we weren't allowed down." She closed her eyes. "I can see him better here than I could there. He's an older man. He's got white hair, a white beard. He's very content."

As Echo spoke, her eyelids twitched and her head moved slightly side to side. "He's pleased with his house—and he does consider it his house. He likes that important people live there, that history is being made there . . . Okay, okay," she added, as if responding to a voice only she could hear. "He doesn't care for the tours. He likes dignitaries, the aristocrats—his word—that come and go."

"Why is he there?" I asked.

"Pride in his home," Echo said, eyes still shut. "He just sits there, often by a window, and he watches people pass by. He's probably the original owner" (Horace Hills Irvine, we learned on the tour, a St. Paul attorney who built the place in 1910). "Uh huh, yes, I see. He also enjoys having a cigar— or two." Echo's eyes popped open. "We should find out if anybody smells cigar smoke when Jesse Ventura is not in the mansion!"

Did she feel the need to ghostbust him?

"Wouldn't do any good," she said, shaking her head. "He's determined to be there. In fact, most ghosts are, well, I don't know if stupid is the right word, but hardheaded. Immature."

As Echo explained it, "Ghosts are like everybody else. They just happen to be dead." Which means they have unresolved issues, they cling to what they know, and they're slow to recognize what's good for them. "In death as in life, we have the freedom of choice," Echo said. "Most of us step into the light, where our souls continue to evolve, but some stay in this world—ghosts. Some are afraid they might go to hell. Others want to remain close to someone here; others have someone they are afraid to see in heaven, like an abusive parent. Some ghosts don't even know they're dead! It's sad because ghosts are stuck, neither in this life nor the afterlife."

The next day was Sunday, and I counted more than 150 open houses listed in the paper. I suggested we pick the neighborhood with the most homes and hit as many as possible. But I'd forgotten who my partner was. "Let me look that over while you enjoy your coffee," Echo said, taking the paper. Fifteen minutes later she'd selected three homes—"the ones I got the strongest feelings about."

Our first stop was a "comfortable starter" in Minneapolis's Richfield section. Before we got out of the car, Echo said, "I think we should look in the basement." We offered a quick hello to the agent as we headed downstairs. In a corner, we found a workbench, above which hung a row of empty baby food jars for nails and screws. "There he is," Echo said.

"Who, where?"

"A spirit—an old, stale spirit, definitely dead—right in front of the bench." She traced a spot in the air. "He spent a lot of time down here when he was alive. He doesn't care about the rest of the house—others claimed that. This was his space."

I looked, I squinted, but I couldn't see a thing.

"He's not here this minute," Echo added. "But his energy is, and it's fresh. He stays here and one other place he likes to spend a lot of time in."

"The American Legion Hall?" I offered.

Echo shot me a startled look. "You're probably right. And there's one nearby!"

At the American Legion Hall, Echo stopped still in the doorway—to adjust her eyes, I assumed, to the cavelike darkness. "Oooh," she said, grimacing, "this place is crawling with vibes." (I noticed something equally disturbing, a flyer by the door that read: "Meat Raffle . . . every Thursday, 6 to 8 P.M.") We bought Cokes at the bar and sat at a table as far from the smoke and strange looks as we could get. After five minutes, we couldn't take it any longer. "Well, no ghosts there," Echo said, gulping fresh air outside. "Just a lot of macho vibes and bravado."

We pulled up in front of a one-and-a-half-story house and stared at it. "Yup, there's a spirit in there," Echo said, still gripping the wheel. "I can feel it. It's a woman. She's on the first floor, in the back, directly beyond the front door. Bet she's in the kitchen."

Damned (so to speak) if we didn't open the door to a hallway that led straight to the kitchen. "She's here," Echo whispered, making a circle in front of the kitchen sink. "It's definitely the spirit of an older woman. Probably a previous owner, now dead."

Touring the house, I tried to tap my own powers. Each room was a showcase of knickknacks, floral prints, and hand-knitted afghans, pillow covers, place mats, and throw rugs. A lace-covered side table displayed a half dozen porcelain religious figures. The television was at least thirty years old. I had to agree with Echo. I, too, detected the spirit of an older woman.

The real-estate agent stopped us at the door. "She's eager to sell," he said. "She's the original owner, and she's reached that point where she can no longer manage the place by herself."

I tried to think of a way of broaching the possibility of a glitch in her reading of the ghost in the kitchen, but before I could, Echo cleared it all up. "Very interesting," she said. "I bet that woman is taking a nap somewhere."

"Huh?"

"When you nap, the soul can leave your body," she explained. "That woman's soul came back to the sink to watch. She's very protective of the house, and I can tell you this—she's not seen any buyers she likes yet."

I'll admit, there's much about the spirit world I don't get. For starters, how consciousness can exist without a living body to feed it. Even more confusing to me is communication with the dead, which entails the living tapping into the "high-frequency vibrations" of the nonliving's "energy." No matter how many times I try to wrap my brain around that cosmology, I always wind up cross-eyed.

Far easier to comprehend is why belief in contact with the beyond has such broad appeal. For those who grieve inconsolably, the impulse to talk to the dead can be irresistible. As Hamlet mourns the murder of his father, the dead king simply appears before his distraught son and speaks with him. After the devastating loss of life in World War I, spiritualism, a movement that was organized in the nineteenth century but based on an old notion that the living and dead can chat, spread like wildfire across Europe and the United States. (In fact, spiritualism has experienced a revival, if you will, after each of our nation's wars, from the Civil War on. Abraham Lincoln's wife, Mary Todd, grew interested in spiritualism during the war, increasingly so after the deaths of her eleven-year-old son, William, and her husband.)

But there are other reasons interest in communicating with the dead rises and falls in cycles. Because it's free of doctrine and is extra-ecclesiastical, spiritualism is hottest at times when, like today, people are turning to individual, rather than institutional, forms of religion and spirituality. On the heels of the nineties angel trend, vastly popular mediums such as bestselling author James Van Praagh and television's John *(Crossing Over)* Edward teach that we can all, to varying degrees, access the spiritual realm ourselves. So why does the appeal of psychics invariably wane? Because not enough happens. The messages mediums relay from the dead are brief and vague, and after a while the living get bored.

Still, before I left, Echo gave me a psychic reading that blew me away—creepily accurate details about my life, my concerns and aspirations, she couldn't have guessed. If she's always that good, she's worth whatever she charges. When I asked how she knew this information, Echo said she channeled it through her spirit guide, Lilli, who had consulted my two spirit guides, Jasper and Charlene, friends from my past lives as a Scottish soldier and a German goat farmer. I'm not sure which stunned me most: that I have spirit guides, that I've had past lives, or that I'm probably the first person in the history of reincarnation who wasn't Leonardo da Vinci or Napoleon.

The last house we visited was an unkempt rambler in south Minneapolis. "I don't like the vibes of this place," Echo said, as we waded across the uncut lawn to the front door. Inside, the house was long and narrow, dark and gloomy. Echo stuck her head into the doorway of the back bedroom and jumped back. "Oh my gosh," she gasped. "There's something terrible in there!" She disappeared around the corner. I looked in and saw a small room, empty except for a bed.

Echo called me down to the basement to explain: "I saw images of violence in that room. Physical, maybe even sexual. Let's go."

The real-estate agent stopped us at the door, and Echo came clean, telling him that she was a psychic drawn to the house by her intuition. To our surprise, the agent replied with total sincerity that he was fascinated by psychic phenomena. He gave Echo his card, saying he knew of some places that might be haunted if she was curious. Then, making sure no one else was around, he asked Echo what she'd found. She said there was something creepy about one of the rooms in the back.

"Oh, I know," he said, nodding. "The bedroom."

Then he added, and I'm not making this up: "That's probably the room in which the old man whacked himself."

Echo and I looked at each other, eyes the size of Frisbees.

"I'm not saying anything happened, of course," he added quickly. "Let's just say there's lots of speculation."

Well, yeah. Speculation was the order of the day. Standing in a grubby subdivision house talking about a guy offing himself in the back room, I realized I'd had my fill and was ready to ferry home across the river Styx. Echo and the real-estate agent had settled in for a long chat. I eased open the screen door and sneaked back to the car to wait.

Laughing at Death

As the hearse glided up to a stoplight, three kids about twelve years old started jumping up and down on the corner. They pointed, waved, and laughed hysterically. One of the kids stepped off the curb and planted his face on the side window. He saw me. I was lying on my back in an open coffin, propped up on a big fluffy pillow. I turned my head to the boy and saluted him. He threw his hands in the air and shrieked with delight.

This was no dream, or nightmare. I was riding in the back of a flamingo pink hearse, laid out in a pink coffin, both the property of the Dying-to-Get-In company. It's a good thing I'm not claustrophobic. The metal casket was narrow and, though I could see over its lacy sides, there was little room between me and the roof of the hearse (which made getting in and out of the coffin tricky). Plus, I was drenched in sweat. It was a hot, muggy summer afternoon, and the hearse's windows were rolled tight as the air-conditioning strained to barely cool just the driver's section. From my corpse's-eye view of downtown Port Washington, New York, I watched as we elicited stares and honks and literally stopped traffic behind us. The theory behind the company is that I was learning to laugh in the face of death, but thus far the spectacle we'd created was teaching me more about handling others' laughing at me.

Dying-to-Get-In is the brainchild of Gerri Guadagno and Gayle Stimler. In addition to offering hearse rides for all occasions, from retirement parties and proms to airport pickups and "even funerals," Gerri and Gayle create customized funeral urns and conduct YOU-logy workshops—self-discovery seminars where participants learn, among other things, how to draft their own eulogies. The two also arrange fun-filled cemetery tours and offer unique ways of dispersing your loved one's ashes, including the "Up, Up and Away" (send a "smattering of ashes" skyward, their website offers, with a cluster of personalized helium balloons) and the "Surf & Turf Combo" ("scatter at sea and save some for land").

On Gerri's business card is inscribed: "Faux Funeral Cortege: Experience It AND Live to Talk About It!" Gerri and Gayle, both in their forties, met at a women's support group in 1992. They say whatever comes across their minds and laugh easily. What made them start Dying-to-Get-In is a simple belief that the key to enjoying life is to adopt an irreverent attitude toward death.

My first question for Gerri was why someone would want to tool around in a hearse. "There's such a stigma about death in our culture," she replied, her voice bubbling with excitement. "We can't even talk about it. And what makes us more uncomfortable than the sight of a big old gloomy black hearse? Well, nothing takes the sting out of that more than a big old fun pink hearse. It's a hoot! Plus," she added, "a ride in a hearse is something very few people experience while they're alive."

While I was mulling her last comment, she convinced me
to come take the pink hearse for a spin.

The house was a cinch to find, just like Gerri said. "Just
look for the pink hearse out front!" Sure enough, there it
was, as hard to miss as an adult elephant. Besides being
friends and business partners, Gerri and Gayle, both divorced,
are roommates who share a cramped but cozy apartment with
two cats above a thrift shop in Port Washington. ("We're
partners, yes," Gerri said, "but we're not 'partners' in that
sense. Just in case you wondered.")

Gerri finalized her divorce in December 2000 and marked
the occasion by legally changing her name from Gerry to
Gerri. "That *i* is significant," she said, "because from now on
it's all about me."

Sitting in their living room, the two women have the antic,
slightly edgy glow of Thelma and Louise, set in Long Island
and crossed with, say, Abbott and Costello. If you haven't
experienced Long Island womanhood, think, especially in
the case of Gayle, of Mike Myers's *Saturday Night Live* character Linda Richman, the one who gets "verklempt."

"A few years ago, I was thinking about my life and my
understanding of death," said Gerri. "And I thought, When
you're gone, what's left of you? For most, it's just a plaque in
a cemetery that bears a name and two dates. And what do we
know about their lives? Nothing. Only that it was a dash
between two dates. I find that appalling. I decided I want to
leave a stronger statement about who I was."

Like what?

"First, I realized I don't want to be interred," Gerri said.
"I want to be cremated. So then it's a question of what to put

my cremains in. A bronze urn? Sorry, I am not a bronze urn. Well, one day I was in a Kay Bee Toy Store, and I found the solution. It was a novelty item. This little toy box that when you press a button, a voice shouts, 'Excuse me, excuse me, excuse me! Can you let me out of here?' Perfect! I decided I would build a large crate—a multimaterial thing, involving various types of wood and ceramics—in which to place my ashes. And the voice, my voice, will say, 'Lemme outta here!'"

"Oh, oh!" cut in Gayle, leaning forward on the couch. "And it must—simply, must—have your laugh! That would be absolutely fabulous."

When I asked Gayle what her final resting place will be, she sighed thoughtfully. "Mine keeps changing. But I've got time, hopefully. One idea is a box of Crayola crayons. Because what best expresses who I am is the notion that if life isn't the color you like, well, pick another color. If you don't like the tree green, fine. Make it blue. There's no such thing as 'you can't.' No such thing as impossible. Life can be anything you want it to be.

"I could also do something with a pair of sparkly red shoes like Dorothy's in *The Wizard of Oz*," Gayle added. "Those shoes become her tool for self-discovery and give her the power and freedom to decide her own fate. At other times, I think, It's not Dorothy's shoes that best express me. It's a nice pair of red stiletto heels!" she said, laughing uncontrollably.

Talk like this is how Gerri, a graphic artist, got the idea of turning customized funeral urns, or "statements," into a business. Students of the three-day, $750 YOU-logy workshops undertake exercises aimed at helping them "explore and re-connect with the person they've always been—before the hardships of life and work intruded, blurring everything."

So often, Gerri said, a person dies, and all the living can think to say is " 'She was a good person,' or 'He was a successful businessman.' How depressing! We're so much more than that." Students are then taught how to express, "celebrate," their essential selves. "It doesn't always have to be a cremains container," Gayle said. "It can be a poem or an essay or a collage."

One student chose to express herself through a miniature metal shopping cart. When she's cremated, her ashes will be placed inside the cart in a shopping bag marked, "Shop Till You Drop." "And until she dies," Gerri said, "she can display the cart on her coffee table. Talk about a conversation piece!"

Another student decided on a handheld vacuum cleaner. "He was very sick and has since passed away," Gayle said. "And on his statement, he wrote, 'Death Sucked the Life Out of Me.' "

"Everyone has a different perspective," Gerri added. "For some, the glass is half full. For others, it's half empty. Either way, death is a fact of life we all have to come to terms with."

For $2,500, Gerri will create a "statement" for you, as she did for a woman whose father recently passed away. "She e-mailed me the request but didn't tell me much about her father except that he always hung out at his neighborhood bar in Far Rockaway. She said he loved Jack Daniel's and always believed, 'There's no party without Jack.'" The daughter wanted the celebratory urn on short notice, in time for the man's wake, a festive Irish wake, to be held at his favorite bar.

"That's all she told us," Gerri said. "So I thought and thought. Finally, I realized, why not a big bottle of Jack Daniel's!"

Gerri managed to secure a rare, three-liter bottle of Jack—"just big enough to hold a glass insert containing his cremains."

Gerri and Gayle delivered the bottle to the wake in the pink hearse. When they pulled up, a crowd awaited them outside. Presented with the bottle, the daughter was shocked. "She loved it," Gerri said. "She was thrilled! She said there was nothing more personal, nothing that could have better captured who her father was."

Then it was time for my joyride in the hearse. Somehow, all our talk about death and remembrance made the prospect of reclining in a pink coffin, just for the fun of it, seem oddly less eccentric. Still, as Gerri held open the rear door for me, the creep factor hit me. It wasn't my mortality that got me; it was everyone who had preceded me. The secondhand 1983 Cadillac DeVille had previously been owned by a Queens funeral home and had ushered thousands of dearly departeds to their final resting place.

I paused. Perhaps sensing my hesitation, Gerri said, "Sorry there's no music in the rear. I'd like to install a stereo," she said, with a straight face. "Gloria Gaynor's 'I Will Survive' would be perfect back there."

I looked at her, laughed, and climbed into the coffin.

The Slough of Despond

Therefore is it called the Slough of Despond: for still as the sinner is awakened about his lost condition, there ariseth in his soul many fears, and doubts, and discouraging apprehensions, which all of them get together, and settle in this place.

My Travels with Uta

First, let me say that I respect and admire Uta Ranke-Heinemann. Granted, her "nervous breakdown" in New York a mere two days into the $20,000 publicity tour the company I worked for had organized to promote the author and her latest book, *Putting Away Childish Things,* did almost send our marketing director into cardiac arrest.* Still, Uta (no one else in our office called her Frau Dr. Ranke-Heinemann, so why should I?) is a widely respected theologian and a bestselling author. Her previous book, *Eunuchs for the Kingdom of Heaven: Women, Sexuality, and the Catholic Church,* had already sold more than a million copies in Europe before it became a runaway bestseller in the United States in 1990—due in no small part to New York's Cardinal John O'Connor, who condemned the book, reportedly without having read it, as "scrawling dirty words about the church on bathroom walls."

I should also mention my own stake in the affair. If it hadn't been for Uta's sudden threat to grab the next flight back to Germany, Harper never would have flown me around the country with her in the hope of salvaging the tour.

---

* This story recounts my experiences working as a publicist at Harper-SanFrancisco.

Instead, I would have passed those two weeks chained to my desk, writing jacket copy and press releases and wondering, as so many publishing professionals do, if I'd ever get to taste the glamorous lifestyles our bestselling authors lead.

When I first met her in her room at the Swissôtel in Boston, Uta was—well, a wreck. Just to open the door was a major undertaking for her. She stood on the other side and kept asking who I was. (Big surprise. I was there at exactly 9:15—the moment we'd agreed I'd fetch her for our first appointment.)

"Who is it?"

"John."

"Room service?"

"No, it's John."

"I don't vont my room cleaned!"

"It's John, from Harper."

"Harper?"

"John Spalding, from HarperSanFrancisco."

"Yes, yes," she said, swinging open the door—pleased, no doubt, to see I wasn't holding a vacuum cleaner. "Right you are. Come in."

She was wearing the smart green leather dress I later learned was the source of her nickname—the Green Lady— given to her by the German press because it's the outfit the sixty-seven-year-old theologian wears at every TV appearance. It was also the only outfit I ever saw her in because it was the only one she'd brought with her. That, two blouses, and the "twenty-five to thirty" pairs of handmade white gloves she always carried with her in a bag. Such minimal travel wear struck me as odd because not only is Uta a successful author but she's also the daughter of the late Gustav Heinemann, president of West Germany from 1969 to 1974.

As I tried to picture Patti Davis on a national author tour with just one dress and a bag of gloves, Uta's voice broke in.

"No matter how many times you tell ze hotel not to clean your room," she informed me at the door, "someone always tries to. Trust no one!"

After an abrupt handshake, Uta was off darting around the room, absently straightening things up and, near tears, explaining to me the events leading to her collapse at the Omni Berkshire in New York.

"Ze doors banged all night long, and I didn't have my sleeping pills. The ambulances—woo! woo!—never stopped. Each night I lay in bed, covered in sweat, my heart pounding like I vas going to die. I phoned my husband, and he told me to come home if Harper didn't send someone. Finally I changed rooms with a nice man, and got my sleeping pills. But never did I sleep one hour in fifty-eight hours. I was persecuted, John! Just persecuted. But the worst part was ze banging of ze doors!"

While I was still puzzling over the banging doors and ambulances, Uta was dragging me into the other room so that I could show her how to turn on the TV—a lesson I would have to repeat at each of our many hotels. Then she handed me all the "inessentials" I was to take charge of: her room keys, plane tickets, and spending money. That done, she sighed, adjusted her wig in the mirror, and marched over to the door. "There ve are, John," she said with sudden calm. "Now ve go?"

"Uh, yeah. Let's go."

"Where are ve going?" she asked.

As I opened the car door for Uta en route to our first stop, she fumbled through her bag and, from among the gloves, produced a large sheet of plastic, which she spread across the seat before hopping in. This she would do everywhere— cars, restaurants, radio stations—and it did not go unnoticed by some of our escorts. Ken Wilson, our escort in Los Angeles, was offended by the plastic sheet. On our second day together he confided to me that he thought Uta's behavior was a nonverbal comment on the condition of his car. (He was right. But it wasn't his car so much as all cars.) That morning he got it washed.

Walking onto the set for her live interview on *Eyewitness News at Noon*, Uta stopped in front of me, handed me her bag, and gave me solemn instructions. "This bag," she said, "you must hold for me. But what is most important is that you do not set it on ze floor. It must stay clean. Do you understand, John?"

"I give you my word. It will not touch the floor."

"Good," she said, spinning around. "Together ve vill accomplish great things."

And during that interview, Uta accomplished a great deal. She explained the highlights of her book: how early Christianity had embellished the life of Jesus with legends and superhuman features. And how these "fairy tales of the kingdom"—the virgin birth, the miracles, Good Friday, Easter, the ascension—had eventually been transformed from simple teaching stories into doctrines to which the church still demands absolute allegiance.

"They put gold all over him," Uta said of Jesus. "They let him walk over ze water, let him change water into wine, let him say to Lazarus, 'Come out,' and all that nonsense. That's, for them, important. I don't care that someone walks over rooftops. I listen to ze words of Jesus!"

As Uta went on about "ze stupidity of local German bishops" and "the pope's mania for virginity," I overheard the set producer, who stood in front of me, whisper urgently into her headset, "Give her more time, more time!" Uta extended the three-minute slot they'd given her to five.

On Friday Uta's spirits were high. She'd finally gotten some sleep and was once again eating well. She gave an interview in her room to *The Providence Journal*. When I arrived shortly with the *Journal*'s photographer, Uta instructed him that, because he was twenty-five years too late to photograph her face, he would have to shoot her legs—"my only beautiful feature left."

All day Uta soared. In interviews she was direct, humorous, brilliant, and full of the controversial one-liners she uses to alert listeners to her subtle arguments. Statements like: "The pope is my theological Mr. Sandman"; "Christians are addicted to blood"; and "Christianity is an education in cruelty." All her interviewers took an immediate, if somewhat baffled, liking to her.

Her last interview of the day completed, Uta invited me to her room to celebrate her triumphs with some cranberry juice. After we clinked glasses, I brought up a topic she had been asked about earlier—the resurrection. Frankly, her response regarding the issue had surprised me. She told the radio station WODS that the resurrection was not one of the Christian "fairy tales" she wanted to debunk—that it was, in fact, the only church claim she did believe in. I found this puzzling, especially since a great influence on her thinking was Rudolf Bultmann, famous for demythologizing the New

Testament. I'd read a lot of Bultmann in college and thought he saw the resurrection as a Christian myth, a metaphor for the possibilities of transformation available to us when we live fully in the present.

"Did Bultmann believe in a literal resurrection, too?" I asked.

"Of course!" Uta said. "In my book I tell you exactly what he told me about ze resurrection."

"I read that," I said. "But his explanation there struck me the same way his writing on the subject did—cryptic."

"Cryptic!" Uta yelped, pointing a finger at me excitedly. "Yes, cryptic. He was cryptic. Right you are!"

Somehow I'd hit the nail right on the head, and the whole issue of life after death was resolved. I was confused, but clearly in her eyes I was now on a higher intellectual plane than I'd been before.

"Wonderful, John!" exclaimed Uta, clapping her hands like a schoolgirl. "And for that you get another cranberry juice. Call room service for two more!" Later I phoned my boss with the good news. Uta was back in the swing of things. My mission was already a success. From here on, the tour would be gravy. But that night something horrible happened.

Uta phoned me at 7:00 A.M. to explain. "Ze sleeping pill would not work. I slept only one hour. Zen, this morning, ze phone rings again! Zey asked if I wanted a vake-up call. Says I, 'Are you crazy?' I slammed the phone. Next hotel, John, we must fix the phones ourselves. You can trust no one. But never mind," she said, sighing deeply. "Today I am ruined and everything is disaster!"

Okay, I thought. This morning we fly to Washington, D.C., with no appointments till Monday. We can deal.

As the plane gently sailed through blue skies for Washington, Uta turned to me and asked, apropos of nothing, "Do you think Swissôtel will be upset with what I did to their phones?"

I was confused. "What did you do to their phones?"

"Ah," she sighed. "I cut ze cords. To teach zem a lesson!"

Uta's room at the Sheraton-Carlton in Washington was all wrong. It was on the eighth floor—the hotel has only eight— so she would hear traffic.

I learned that at the Omni in New York—where the ambulances ruined her sleep—Uta was on the twenty-fifth floor. (Incidentally, I also learned then that in addition to the port and sleeping pills Uta takes before bed, she wears earplugs.)

We examined her room. Uta counted four doors in the hall outside hers. Despite this serious handicap, we started preparing her suite. We had room service bring up two blankets and mineral water, and Uta stripped the bed; she needs heavy blankets and hates those flimsy hotel bedspreads. We called the engineer to have the bathroom phone dismantled. I unplugged the two remaining phones and the fax machine and moved the alarm clock from the bedroom to the living room, where, as instructed, I wrapped the cord snugly around the clock for good measure. We pulled the drapes so as not to allow even a ray of light into the room and turned the air-conditioning on high (another personal bête noire— heat), and I showed Uta how to use the television, though most of her attention seemed focused on orchestrating the confusion mounting in the room.

When the electrician entered the bedroom and stumbled into the guy from room service, I thought that all we needed was a maid and a concierge to walk in and we'd have the crowded cabin scene from the Marx Brothers' *A Night at the Opera*.

Once she was settled and the hotel personnel had left, Uta decided at last that the room would not do. I reminded her that they'd given her the only suite available. She panicked. "Zen ve must go to another hotel."

I told Uta to calm down and that I'd go back to the desk and see what I could do. Again I was told there simply were no other suites. I asked for the phone numbers of area hotels. A few minutes later the guy from the desk returned with a list, warning me that it was extremely unlikely I would find another suite anywhere in the city—especially on a Saturday afternoon. Then he said, "Wait a minute," and started checking the computer. "There is a suite I can give you, but it's booked from Monday on." Which meant that after Sunday we'd be on our own till Wednesday. That was fine. I'd bought us some time, and Uta needn't know our predicament. I'd figure something out.

As I was taking the keys, Uta came rushing to the desk in hysterics, all packed and ready to leave. "John, John," she screamed, "we must leave now or else I go back to Germany. I heard ze doors bang!" Back upstairs, the deskman helped me move Uta to her new room, commenting grudgingly that there was no way he could rebook the room that day.

That night Uta slept well. So well, in fact, that she called me at 7:00 A.M. the next day inviting me to go for a walk.

"When?" I grumbled.

"I'm ready now," she chirped.

Later that evening I ran into the guy from the desk in the lobby. He gave me the best news I'd had all day. The director of booking had happened by earlier, and the desk clerk had convinced him to move the woman taking Uta's suite the next day into another suite. Back in my room, I did a little dance.

The next thing I knew, it was 6:30 Monday morning, and my phone was ringing. It was Uta. She said she had blood poisoning.

"What do you mean, you've got blood poisoning?"

"Blood poisoning, John." She moaned. "My shoe cut my heel on our walk, and I'm going to have blood poisoning, which my husband almost died of before I left Germany. They were going to have to operate, zen ze doctor gave him a prescription. You must call a doctor and get me some penicillin at once or else it vill spread up my leg and attack my heart."

What could I say? I rushed right over. Of course, it was just a small blister, and I told her so. I went downstairs and bought some Band-Aids and alcohol pads. This calmed her. Then she dropped the bomb. "John," she said, "ve must leave zis hotel immediately."

"Oh?" I inquired casually. "Why must we leave immediately?"

"Because of ze traffic," she explained. "It kept me up all night and now I am once again ruined.

"Back where I was in New York with ze banging of ze doors, no sleep, and my head completely in the fogs!"

I knew exactly what she was talking about. An author tour is hard on anyone. The planes, the cars, the new cities, the long hours—it was all beginning to catch up with me, too. So I gave in. Uta needed her rest, and I needed mine. The next morning, while Uta gave interviews, I phoned hotels. Miraculously, the Park Hyatt had an open suite, and when Uta returned to the Carlton at noon, I was waiting in the lobby with our luggage.

Hands down, Uta's best interview of the tour occurred the following day with Hollis Engley of Gannett News Service. Before Hollis arrived, I was with Uta in her room waiting for his call. The day before, we'd had the engineer up to take apart the bathroom phone. It lay in about seven pieces on the bathroom floor.

When Hollis called, the only phone that rang was the one in the bathroom. I went down to the lobby to get Hollis. When we returned to the room, Uta was in hysterics about the phone and greeted the Gannett reporter with a lecture on the inefficiency of hotels. She told him about New York, the traffic, cutting the phone cords, and her sleeping pills. As she rattled on, Hollis shot me a bewildered glance. I shrugged my shoulders.

The interview under way, Uta quickly turned her criticism to the Roman Catholic creed. "What does it say about ze life of Jesus? Only zat he was 'born of the Virgin Mary, was crucified and buried.' In between is not interesting for Christians, because he said something—love your enemies—zey do not want to hear. Zey care only about zat fairy tale for children five years old—the Virgin Mary and redemption by blood. Zey can't live without blood. Zey vont to be redeemed by blood, the death penalty, and military retaliation. Jesus may as well have sat at home all thirty-three years doing nothing but crossword puzzles. Doesn't matter."

Hollis wrote furiously in his notebook.

Uta explained that she became the world's first woman professor of Catholic theology when she was given a church-appointed chair at the University of Essen. In 1987 the church declared her ineligible to teach, after she pronounced the virgin birth a theological belief and not a biological fact. Today she's still on the faculty at Essen but holds a state-appointed chair.

"How many languages are you fluent in?" Hollis asked.

"Twelve," Uta replied, placing English seventh in her level of competence, after Russian, Polish, Spanish, Italian, French, and German. At the end of the interview Uta said, "Now, Hollis, you must take a look at my bathroom phone. Perhaps you can fix it."

"Why not?" he said.

There was Hollis Engley, sitting on Uta's bathroom floor, legs wrapped around the toilet, stuffing toilet paper between the ringer and bell, when suddenly he seemed to realize what he was doing. He paused and looked up at Uta and me. "You know," he said, laughing, "I'm about to go back to my office and tell everyone that I spent the afternoon with a world-famous theologian, sitting on the toilet fixing her phone!" At the door he asked Uta for a hug, and I then escorted him to the lobby.

When I returned to Uta's room, she was trying to figure out how to turn on the air-conditioning. Taking over the knob, I caught Uta from the corner of my eye. She looked as pleased with herself as ever I'd seen her.

"Happy with the interview?" I asked.

"Oh yes," she said, poking at her wig in the mirror. "I think zat scene in ze bathroom will provide ze color his story needs."

That evening held our final event in D.C.—a signing at Borders Book Store in North Bethesda, Uta's first on the tour.

She didn't complain when only fifteen people attended. She didn't even seem to notice; she was too excited that there were some fundamentalists in the audience. Until then she hadn't encountered any on the tour, and I think she was a little disappointed. After her twenty-minute talk the fundamentalists opened fire. Uta thrived on the antagonism, responding to their accusations of heresy with questions they couldn't answer. One young zealot stood up and blurted, "Do you deny the Bible's claim that Mary was a virgin?" Uta cut him short. "Are you crazy? Of course I do! The church is always so concerned about ze harm done to its religious feelings, but what about ze harm it does to my religious intellect?" Her inquisitor stared at her blankly as she explained how Christianity had merely adopted the virgin birth from the same ancient pagan legends used to establish the divinity of everyone from Heracles and Asclepius to Alexander the Great and Caesar Augustus. The Q & A period over, Uta signed the store's stock of books with zest.

We checked into our hotel in Chicago—another Swissôtel, I might add—at 5:00 P.M. When we turned the key and walked into Uta's room on the thirty-eighth floor, our Chicago escort, Tip Walker, Uta, and I let out a collective gasp. Before us was a two-floor suite, with a cathedral ceiling and a winding staircase to the bedroom, and a door on each level. Downstairs were a living room, kitchen, dining room, and study area complete with a huge wood desk. There were two bathrooms. The minibar was the size of a bank vault. This must have been a mistake. "Finally!" Uta cried. "A hotel room I deserve. Now I live like an oil sheikh!"

I also counted four telephones, two alarm clocks, and a fax machine—all of which we promptly disconnected, enlisting the help of an engineer with the phones in the bathroom. (Later I learned that the hotel had made a mistake. Since they'd put someone else in the room they'd booked for Uta, they made up for the error by shifting her into this nine-hundred-dollar-a-night luxury suite.) From upstairs Uta yelled down, "John, call your office and tell them I am very content viz ze room! Things are looking better all ze time!"

Tip went downstairs to move the car, saying she'd be up in fifteen minutes to collect us for Uta's interview at CRIS radio. Unpacking in my room, I suddenly realized that Uta—phoneless and ensconced on the second level of her palace—would never hear our knock. Sure enough, she didn't. Although I had Uta's room key, she always chained the door after I left. Through the crack I shouted, but to no avail. I ran upstairs and banged on the door that led down a long hall to Uta's bedroom. Still nothing. Tip suggested maybe Uta had fallen down the staircase and broken her neck. Ten minutes passed. We were now running late for our interview. I told Tip to check the lobby, in case Uta had misunderstood us. I kept banging on the door. Finally I went down to the lobby, hoping Tip had had better luck. She hadn't. When we returned to Uta's door, I hit it harder. Suddenly the door opened, and Uta gave us a cold stare. "Where have you two been?" she said, hand on hip, checking her watch. "You said fifteen minutes. I vaited for you in my bed now one half hour. Surely ve are late!"

Uta had finally got what she wanted—a room so silent, so inaccessible, that absolutely nothing could disturb her. She didn't seem to understand, however, that now even I—the one she depended on completely to help her negotiate her rounds—couldn't reach her.

Ernst-Ulrich Franzen from the *Milwaukee Journal Sentinel* was supposed to call at 10:00 the next morning. Uta was supposed to plug in her bedroom phone at 9:45. I was to call her at 9:50 and then walk over. Of course, at 9:45 Uta's phone was still unplugged. At ten till, I banged on her door. Nothing. Five minutes later I got a maid to unlock the upstairs door, although it was still predictably chained shut. I tried shouting through the crack. Remarkably, this time Uta heard me and screamed, "John, where are you?"

"Upstairs," I yelled.

"I'm coming, John. I'm coming."

I waited. Then I realized she misunderstood and went to the door downstairs. By the time I got there, it was locked and bolted again. After several herculean slams, Uta came to the door.

"Where vere you?" she cried. "I heard you, then you weren't there ven I vent for you."

"Never mind," I said, rushing for the desk to plug in the phone. As I did, it rang. It was Ernst.

After that interview I set the phone up so Uta could do her eleven o'clock taped interview with Ron Way (of ABC Radio's *An Eye on Faith*) from bed—where she prefers to conduct all phone interviews, because she can rest her feet on a hot water bottle. When Ron called, I handed the phone to Uta (now perched on her pillows) and returned to my room for a nap.

Twenty minutes later, my phone rang. It was Ron Way.

"John, is that you?" he asked.

"Ron?" I answered. "Why are you calling me? Aren't you interviewing Uta?"

"I was," he said, "then there was a crash, then silence, and now I can't reach her."

"Did it ruin your taping?" I asked, having now become the purest of pragmatists.

"I can fix it," he said. "But, boy, is she a pistol!"

I asked Ron to give me five minutes. Back in Uta's suite I ran upstairs, where I found her sitting in bed, laughing hysterically. The phone was all over the floor. Picking up the pieces, I asked what had happened.

"I don't know!" Uta roared. "I got up to get some water, and next zing I know I'm all tangled in ze cord and it crashes in a million pieces on ze floor, as you see. Zen," she continued, controlling herself, "I pick up ze phone, and say 'Ron?'

"I hear, 'Hotel operator, how may I help you?'

"Says I, 'No, I vont ze radio station!'

"Says she, 'Which radio station, ma'am?'

"Says I, 'I don't know, ask John!' Then I hang up!"

Uta was laughing so hard over this incident that I feared for her health. I fixed the phone, and shortly Ron called back. Still laughing, Uta took the receiver and said, "Ron? You won't believe vat happened!"

I got out of there fast.

Morton Downey, Jr., swaggered into the waiting room at Major Networks, Inc., in Chicago and took Uta's hand. "And

you must be the one and only Uta Rrrrranker-Heinemann,"
he said, exaggerating his *r*'s for comic effect. Well, I thought,
too late to leave now.

Although Downey used Uta's presence to deliver his own
blasts at Catholicism, rarely letting her get a word in edge-
wise, he repeatedly instructed his listeners to go out and buy
her book. "It's absolutely brilliant. It will challenge the way
you think," he said. "It will open your mind and actually
strengthen your faith!"

Uta played Downey perfectly. When he asked if she had
children, she said yes. When he asked, "Boys, girls?" She
said, "Two sons." When he asked if they were conceived by the
Holy Spirit, she smiled and said no, adding, "And I von't tell
you how they were conceived, either!" He laughed, leaned
back, and plugged the book again. Then it was off to California.

Nothing in L.A. shook Uta, except her constant fear of
earthquakes. Saturday morning Uta and I had breakfast
together. She'd just finished a two-hour phone interview, and
there was nothing left for us to do but eat and go to the airport.
In the silence, as we finished our croissants and tea, I wondered if Uta was trying to muster up something touching to say
to me. Something simple, of course, like how much she'd
enjoyed our travels together. Or how, if ever I was in Essen, I
should feel free to look her up. Instead, she said something
more endearing—and a whole lot more practical—than that.

"Be sure to take that marmalade viz you when you leave,"
she said, pointing with her spoon at the unopened jars.
"After all, Harper has paid for them. You are just like my
own sons. Never thinking of zese things.

"Now ve go?"

Fear and Trepanation

"Watch this, watch this!" said Pete Halvorson over a high-pitched whir coming from the TV. "When the doctor pulls the drill out of the skull you're going to get a good look straight into the third eye!"

Halvorson was showing me one of the four cranial operations he filmed at a hospital in Mexico. I don't consider myself particularly squeamish, but I found myself glancing away from the TV. I hoped Pete didn't think I was bored.

As I turned back to the screen, the whirring stopped, the surgeon removed the drill, and a nurse suctioned away the blood and bone fragments. What I saw was a hole that went clear through the skull and stopped just shy of the brain's protective membrane. What Halvorson saw was nothing less than history in the making: a trepanation surgery, performed to help a patient expand her consciousness, and performed at her own request.

Trepanation dates back to the Stone Age. It was practiced by physicians of the ancient world for light head wounds and in the Middle Ages to release evil spirits. But modern Western medicine frowns on trepanation (except to relieve pressure on the brain, after which the piece of skull is replaced), and no doctor in the United States or Western Europe will seriously discuss it, much less perform it, as an elective procedure.

Halvorson, a fifty-seven-year-old jewelry designer whose own trepanation hole is visible as a dent in his mostly bald head, believes trepanation can dramatically improve the quality of life for 80 percent of all adults. The benefits he cites include increased mental abilities, more energy and drive, and a heightened self-awareness and keener perception of reality. He also believes trepanation can help cure depression, stress-related diseases, even multiple sclerosis.

Just a few months prior to my visit, after years of searching, Pete had finally found Dr. David Kirsch in Monterrey, Mexico, who was willing to perform the operation. Eventually, he says, the hospital will accommodate the hundreds of requests Pete receives through his website (www.trepan.com). "This is just the beginning," Pete says. "My long-term goal is to make trepanation available at every outpatient clinic around the world, so that no one will ever have to do what I was forced to do."

In his early twenties, Pete grew distressed over changes in his life—changes some would count as the trappings of adulthood. He felt lethargic, depressed, and disconnected. His studies, once a joy, became a chore. "I could barely read through a single page." After dropping out of college Pete, like many young people in the late sixties, embarked on a "quest for expanded consciousness."

In Amsterdam, he met Bart Huges, a former medical student at the University of Amsterdam who had written a book called *Trepanation: A Cure for Psychosis*. Huges, who since the early sixties had been advocating the procedure as a means to permanently increase one's consciousness, had developed a following and attracted publicity ("most of it," Pete says, "was in the tabloids and inaccurate").

In 1972, the twenty-seven-year-old Halvorson sat in a small room in Amsterdam before an array of bandages, a hypodermic containing the anesthetic Xylocaine, a scalpel, a drill, and four bits. Then, as he'd practiced countless times, he numbed his scalp, made an incision, and, hands above head, bored a three-eighths-inch hole into his skull. He ran the electric drill by a foot pedal, while watching in a mirror. There was a lot of smoke and blood, which he deflected from his eyes with a tent around his face. The procedure took about an hour. "The first thing I noticed was a sense of euphoria," he recalled. "It's an intense high, a sense of happiness and well-being, nothing wild like LSD. And it's a permanent high that never goes away.

"It's as if somebody suddenly turns on a light," he added, "and you realize, Wow, I've been in the dark all this time! It's the opening of the third eye."

The concept of the third eye goes back to ancient Hindu literature, Halvorson says. "The third eye of Shiva was a source of wisdom and illumination, depicted as a fountain coming out of his head. Trepanation was prevalent in those days as a religious practice, and the notion of opening the third eye was a literal reference to trepanation. But over the years the third eye became ritualized and interpreted as a metaphor."

If much of this sounds like a cross between hippie rap and New Age human potential theory, Pete is ready with a lengthy discourse on things like brain pulsations and brain metabolism. He pores over graphs, charts, articles, and other data he has amassed in the hope of convincing the medical profession to take trepanation seriously.

The idea behind the procedure is that a trepanned head gives the brain more room to pulse with each heartbeat, feeding more oxygen to the brain's cells. The hole acts like the soft spot, or fontanel, in a baby's skull, which, Halvorson says, increases the "brain-blood volume" and the brain's ability to function.

By adulthood, Pete says, our skulls have hardened and sealed, restricting the volume of blood in our brains. "That's why so many of us experience a major downer after our teens," he says. "Unfortunately, most people spend the rest of their lives as couch potatoes heading on a downward spiral."

Chris Emery, a fifty-five-year-old American, whom I'd seen under the drill on Pete's videotape from Mexico, told me she decided to get trepanned after years of struggling with depression. "After the surgery I noticed a big difference in my energy levels and outlook on life," she says. "Whereas I used to wake up, walk to the kitchen, and have to sit and rest for a while, I now get up, make my coffee, and get to work." About the fifteen-minute procedure, she said, "It was nothing. I actually fell asleep during it. I'd rather get trepanned than go to the dentist any day!"

The world, of course, is full of people who lead happy, productive lives without drilling holes in their heads. According to Halvorson, many successful people—leaders in business, science, politics, and education, artists and musicians—are "third-eyers." Which means that either (a) their intercranial seams never closed with age (approximately 10 percent of the population) or (b) they sustained a head injury that never fully healed (another 10 percent).

"Take Hitler," Pete says. "In World War I he was trepanned after sustaining a major head wound, like a one-and-a-half-to two-inch hole. Unfortunately, he was a sociopath who used his genius for evil." A hole in the head—well, that's certainly one way to account for Hitler's atrocities.

In a 1998 *Washington Post* article, scientists dismissed the claims for trepanation, saying that brain function depends on blood flow, not blood volume. Even if trepanation did increase the blood flow, they said, there's no evidence that it would increase brain function.

When I asked Pete about the *Post* piece, he replied, "Doctors have a selective hearing disorder. We've never said that trepanation affects blood flow to the brain. We're saying it increases blood volume in the brain, and these doctors have absolutely no data about blood volume because there's never been a single U.S. medical investigation into any aspect of elective trepanation."

Which is why Pete is so thrilled about his association with Dr. Kirsch and his team in Mexico. By giving each patient an MRI before and after the procedure, as well as six months later, Pete hopes he can offer conclusive proof that trepanation increases the brain-blood volume. Psychological evaluations, he says, will demonstrate that trepanation improves brain function.

Pete, who lives on a forty-acre farm in semirural Wernersville, Pennsylvania, was planning to escort a second group of fifteen people to Mexico. The procedure costs

$2,500, and Pete says he doesn't see a dime of it. The only money he makes through trepanation is in the sale of T-shirts and videos offered on his website, which he says barely covers his costs. "My only interest is helping people change their lives through trepanation," he says.

Before ushering them south of the border, Pete says, he insists they get "engrammed," which involves copying and reciting into a tape ten times some literature Pete has prepared on the procedure—"so they fully understand the choice they're making." After trepanation, he recommends they take the Creative Intelligence Program, a "one-on-one training program to evolve human potential," created by Pete's colleague, Jack Krueger, "an artist and third-eyer." "We don't merely want to change people from being unhappy couch potatoes to being happy couch potatoes," Pete says. "We want them to realize their own unique brilliance and to develop their personalities to the fullest."

Most doctors maintain that if a person notices any changes after trepanation, it's probably due to the placebo effect. "Okay, suppose it is just the placebo effect," Pete replies. "Can you tell me what are the medical benefits of face-lifts and breast implants? Talk about the placebo effect! And these procedures are far more risky than trepanation, yet plenty of doctors are willing to perform them."

The Shocking Truth
About John Wesley

Even the most devout Methodists will be excused if they've never considered what their denomination's founder's kitchen looks like. I have stood in it. I was on a tour of the John Wesley House and Museum of Methodism in London, England, and in my ears were the voices of James Rogers, a preacher who lived in the Wesley home, and Elizabeth "Betsy" Ritchie, John Wesley's housekeeper.

All right, what I heard was only actors playing Rogers and Betsy on the audiocassette tour. But to one like me who spent his youth fidgeting in Methodist and Holiness church pews, the house is entrancing. In a room off John Wesley's kitchen are display cases containing his personal belongings—christening robe and baby rattle; his nightcap, shoes, and traveling case, containing the holy man's fork and fruit knife—relics displayed with such reverence it's hard to believe Protestants were involved. "The one on the far right has a very special meaning for me," Rogers said of one cabinet. "It's a lock of the Reverend Mr. Wesley's hair, cut after his death from his poor, dear head and given me." After a pause, Reverend Rogers added solemnly, "Please, take as much time as you want to look at this cabinet, and when you're finished, switch the tape guide on again."

Wesley moved into his four-story Georgian town house in 1779, a year after he built his famous chapel—the "Cathedral of Methodism"—next door. The house stands on City Road in what's now the London Borough of Islington. Wesley, a dissenter from the Church of England, chose a location beyond the old city wall on a site that, ironically, had been used some one hundred years earlier as a dirt dump during the construction of St. Paul's Cathedral about a mile south. Before my visit I stopped to pay respects at Bunhill Fields, the small nonconformist burial ground across the street from Wesley's house. Those buried on the quiet, tree-shrouded grounds include Daniel Defoe, William Blake, George Fox (founder of the Quakers), Susanna Wesley (John and Charles's mother), and John Bunyan. Bunyan's monument is perhaps the largest and most elaborate of the bunch. It includes an effigy of the writer and bas-relief sculptures of scenes from *The Pilgrim's Progress*. In 1898 Wesley's house was opened to the public, and the Museum of Methodism, established in the chapel crypt in 1984, boasts "one of the world's largest collections of Wesleyan ceramics and some of the finest Methodist paintings."

One of these paintings is the now-famous Robert Hunter portrait of Wesley, which he cherished as one of the finest of him ever rendered—"a most striking likeness," he wrote in his journal. But what Wesley didn't mention was that the portrait, painted when he was sixty-two, makes him appear thirty years younger.

Wesley's pinkness is attributable to what Betsy kindly described as "Mr. Wesley's abiding interest in health." Interest, in the days when every medical procedure was an experiment, is a bit of an understatement. In the dining room is displayed Wesley's "chamber horse"—an exercise chair with a thick leather cushion filled with air, which, when sat in, flattened like an accordion. Wesley hopped up and down in this chair for hours, simulating horseback riding. Betsy said, "He was convinced that a due degree of exercise was essential for health and long life. Walking was the best form, followed by riding. He loved exercise, even in old age, and was physically fit!" (A docent told me Wesley often paced his bedroom, having calculated that two hundred trips wall-to-wall equaled a mile.)

In other words, John Wesley was a health nut. "I am as strong at eighty-one as I was at twenty-one," he wrote, "but abundantly more healthy, being a stranger to the headache, toothache and other bodily disorders which attended me in my youth."

This was no secret to his contemporaries. As part of his social ministry, Wesley himself manufactured and dispensed medicine at the Foundery. For this, he was labeled a quack. As one satirist wrote:

> *Tottenham's the best accustom'd Place,*
> *There Magus squints men into Grace,*
> *W—s—y sells Powders, Draughts, and Pills,*
> *Sov'reign against all sorts of Ills.*

Wesleyan theology has no grips on me any longer. But being "follicularly challenged," I couldn't resist trying Wesley's cure for hair loss: "Rub the part morning and evening with onions, till it is red; and rub it afterwards with honey." After several attempts, all I wound up with were onion tears streaming down my face and a sticky, raw forehead that attracted flies.

For lethargy, Wesley recommended "strong vinegar up the nose." And I must say, the vinegar certainly perked me up, as I spent several minutes gagging, spitting, and discharging my nasal cavity into a paper towel.

Primitive Physic: An Easy and Natural Method of Curing Most Diseases was Wesley's main tome on health, which he published in 1747. By its twenty-fourth edition, in 1792, the book included thousands of therapies, many of which Wesley tried himself, noting, sensibly, "Tried" after each. For example, his cure for an earache: "Put in a roasted fig, or onion, as hot as may be: Tried. Or, blow the smoke of tobacco strongly into it." And his cure for a toothache: "Be electrified through the teeth: Tried."

On the house tour, which begins in the basement kitchen, Betsy explains in a prim but exuberant British accent that only plain meals were prepared—"for Mr. Wesley decreed that all pickled, smoked, or salted food, and all high-seasoned, is unwholesome!"

Perfectly wholesome to Wesley, but grounds to expel the old man from most evangelical colleges in America, was relishing fine wines. "I remember how vexed he was," Rogers murmured in my ear, "when a case of claret shipped to him as a gift was seized by customs and, despite several written requests, was never released to him." To think—the man whose teachings form the doctrinal core of, for example, the teetotaling Church of the Nazarene, himself tippled with the devil.

But an even greater shock, so to speak, awaited me upstairs.

Against the rear wall in one room stood a contraption that looked like it belonged more in Dr. Frankenstein's laboratory than in the Reverend Mr. Wesley's study—his "personal electric-shock machine." He'd turn the crank on this crude device to generate a current of electricity through a metal rod, against which he'd press his tongue, forehead, or an ailing body part—a burn or a sore tooth, for example. In the postscript to *Primitive Physic,* Wesley wrote that, of all his cures, "one, I must aver from personal knowledge, grounded on a thousand experiments, to be far superior to all other medicines I have known; I mean Electricity."

Wesley claimed electricity was "the nearest [to a] universal medicine of any yet known in the world" and maintained it could cure almost fifty ailments, from deafness and leprosy to stomachaches and even "feet violently disordered." When his brother, Charles, the famous composer of more than six thousand hymns, lay on his deathbed, John "earnestly advised him to be electrified. Not shocked but only filled with electric fire." Understandably, Charles never roused himself long enough to undergo his brother's cure.

I refrain from criticizing Wesley for his superstitions about electric shock only because I share his preoccupations utterly. I'm with him when he fell sick in 1753 and, convinced he would die any day of "consumption" at age fifty, composed his own epitaph "to prevent vile panegyric." He went on to live another thirty-eight years.

The great success of the John Wesley House is that here the founder of Methodism comes alive, not as the abstract holy man perhaps some followers imagine him to have been, but as a very human person who grappled with the mortal fears we all share. But the museum also illustrates how Wesley addressed those concerns as a mandate to take time seriously, and to order his life so that he could fully realize the ministry he felt called to create. Methodism, I realized as never before, was as much about the ascetic, yes, methodical lifestyle advocated by Wesley, a man who was asleep every night by 9:30 and awake every morning by 4:00, as it was a form of Protestant theology.

"Perhaps the regularity of his life, and the fact that he took regular exercise, helped him age gracefully," observed James Rogers, driving the stake further into me, a guy whose sleep, dietary, and exercise habits are about as regular as flash flooding in the Mojave Desert. To which Betsy added, in a tone that made me want to hire a housekeeper, "He looked wonderful, too. His step was firm and his appearance, to within a few years of his death, was vigorous and muscular. His face was one of the finest I have ever seen—a clear, smooth forehead, an aquiline nose, an eye the brightest and most piercing that can be conceived, and a freshness of complexion scarcely even to be found at his years and expressive of the most perfect health."

Gee, maybe I'll search eBay for an electric-shock machine.

I'm Dreaming of
a Blue Christmas

It was the huge Christmas wreath on the Range Rover's grille that made me hesitate. I was sitting in the parking lot behind a quaint New England downtown shopping center, my signal blinking as I waited for a Honda to leave. Then the Range Rover pulled up from the other direction. As the sedan backed out, the SUV, bearing Christmas on its front, roared into my spot. Slamming the door on her suburban tank, the driver lowered her sunglasses and shot me a Serial Mom stare that would deep-freeze Heatmiser.

Happy Holidays! In this wondrous and magical season, common courtesy is dropped and ruthlessness is tolerated as part of the price we pay to celebrate the birth of Christ. In response, many of us turn to inspirational tales of redemption and altruism to buck up our Christmas spirit. Alice Gray's *Christmas Stories for the Heart,* a compilation of traditional, uplifting holiday tales, is the kind of thing we read to make us think Christmas is worth the fuss because, beneath all the chaos and excess, it's fundamentally about warmth and kindness.

"The Legend of the Robin" tells how Mary, on Christmas Eve, coaxed the stable animals into stoking the fire for her. The horse, ox, and donkey were no help. Then a little brown bird swooped down and fanned the smoldering coals till the bird's chest glowed and a flame ignited—in the coals, that is. "'Dear bird,' Mary said, 'thank you so much for your thoughtfulness. From now on, you will always wear a breast of red as a sign of the kindness in your heart.'"

As touching as that story may be, notice that it's not about the kindness of people at Christmas but about the kindness of animals. Don't forget: The reason Mary and Joseph had to shack up with the animals in the first place was that no human would grant them shelter.

In fact, ask most people to describe a Christmas they'll never forget, and they'll tell you a horror story. A former bank branch manager in my town recalls a Christmas Eve more than twenty years ago: "About an hour before closing, this guy tried to cash a stolen social security check. I refused, and he started shouting obscenities. When I threatened to call the police, he left. I thought that was the end of it. But as I drove home, a car rammed me at a stoplight. In the rearview mirror, I saw the guy from the bank. Next thing I know, he yanked my door open. He swung at me with a crowbar but hit the doorframe. Then he pummeled me with his fist before running back to his car and speeding off. My face was bruised, cut, and swollen, and I had a terrible headache. I stayed awake all night, fearing I had a concussion. On Christmas morning, I finally let my wife, eight months pregnant, drive me to the emergency room."

Or this: "I always work the insane holiday rush," a store manager told me, "so by the time I'd closed up that Christmas Eve I was exhausted. With no family, Christmas was just going to be me and Tawny, my springer spaniel. At thirteen, her eyes were bad, her hearing was going, and her hip was a mess, but she was a sweet old girl. As I turned into my drive, there she was, standing up by the garage, wagging her tail, excited I was home. As I drove up the incline, she limped down to greet me. Suddenly, she slipped on the ice and fell under the car. Unable to stop, I ran over her."

Take these not as gratuitously cruel stories for Yule: Let them be your insurance for an upbeat Christmas. The only way to survive the holiday season is to accept that it's like the rest of the year, except that, as "The Twelve Days of Christmas" reminds us, it's a time made insufferable by an annoying litany of bloated expectations and ridiculous obligations. As Shakespeare says in *All's Well That Ends Well,* "Oft expectation fails, and most oft there/Where most it promises." Translation: If Martha Stewart has you believing you can achieve nirvana if you turn enough toilet-paper tubes into festive tree ornaments, you may be setting yourself up for disappointment.

How can we temper our expectations and salvage our sanity this Christmas? Leave off your thoughts of sugarplums, and drop your copy of Mary "Angelscribe" Ellen's *A Christmas Filled with Miracles: Inspiring Stories for the Magic of the Season* ("Amazing true stories [that] will touch your heart, awaken your memories of Christmas past, and offer you hope for every Christmas to come").

Instead, I recommend Raymond Carver's short story "A Serious Talk," in which a vodka-swilling husband attempts to apologize to his estranged wife and kids for trying to torch the house on Christmas night. Rather than making amends, however, he winds up cutting the phone cord when a caller asks to speak with his wife's "friend" Charlie.

I don't know about you, but my holidays are looking rosier already.

A Pilgrim's Dreams

As I walked through the wilderness of this world, I lighted on a certain place, where was a den; and I laid me down in that place to sleep: and as I slept I dreamed a dream.

Conversations with God
. . . in a Sports Bar

Does God care? Evidently, he's cared sixteen times, because we won sixteen games, and not to say he didn't care the other two times, but maybe he cared enough to allow the other team to win the other two times.

—QUARTERBACK RANDALL CUNNINGHAM

DATE: SUNDAY, NOVEMBER 14, 1999
PLACE: PARK AVENUE COUNTRY CLUB, A SPORTS BAR
    IN MANHATTAN

Q: Excuse me—God?

A: The one and only. Are you surprised?

Q: No, no. I guess I just didn't expect to see you—the supreme deity, that "than which nothing greater can be conceived"—dressed in Nikes and a Super Bowl XXXIII sweatshirt.

A: Well, there's a lot people don't know about me. Hang on! [Points to a TV monitor] It's third and ten with seventeen seconds left to the half. The Giants could take the lead. . . .

C'mon, Big Blue! . . . Gimme a break! I saw great-grand-mothers cross the Red Sea with more hustle! . . . Anyway. Grab a stool. What you drinking?

Q: Uh, whatever you're having.

A: Bartender! Two more, and easy on the ice this time. . . . Great place, eh? Two satellite dishes, ten giant screens, *fifty* TV sets. I can watch all my games, plus I can fire up a stogie and no one complains.

Q: [Waving away smoke] First, Lord, thanks for agreeing to this interview.

A: Sure, just remember what I said. Rule number one: We only talk football. Stick to pigskin, and I'm all yours. Till halftime's over, of course! [Laughs]

Q: Of course. But if I may, why won't you discuss the "big issues"—war, poverty, justice, suffering, the problem of evil . . .

A: Boooring. [Rises and shouts] Hey, anybody want to discuss suffering and the problem of evil? We got ourselves a philosopher over here! [Laughs, sits down] Looks like I'm not the only one who's not biting today, Aristotle.

Q: Right, then. Football it is. When did you become so interested in the NFL?

A: Three, four years ago. That's when I started getting tens of thousands of prayers, every day, from football players. "God, heal my shoulder for next Sunday." "Lord, please, trade me from the Saints, or at least tack another ten mil on my contract." "God, if you put another seven points on the board, we promise . . ." *Lots* of Faustian stuff. And after a game, an entire team would get on its knees on national television and thank *me* for the win! And I thought, Do these guys really think I care who wins a stupid football game? So I started watching the sport, just for kicks. But you know what? The intensity, the athleticism, the bloodlust, John Madden's commentary—suddenly I understood all the fuss. And now I'm hooked. . . . Hey, it's the NASDAQ Halftime Report! Let's see how my Skins are doing.

Q: Looks like Tennessee's up by four.

A: Aw, nuts! Oakland is crushing Miami. Not even *I* saw that coming. . . . Where were we?

Q: Earlier last year, Deion Sanders said, "When it's fourth down, I pray. I'm seeking God's help." He also prays that opposing quarterbacks will throw him the ball. Do you actually intervene in games, say, by giving an athlete a boost of energy or by forcing an interception?

A: Well, I try not to spoil the fun. But, yeah—guilty as charged! Look, I'm like any other fan. I've got my favorites. Difference is, I'm omnipotent. Don't tell me there isn't a Jets fan out there who wouldn't blow a little extra wind behind a Ray Lucas pass—if he could.

Q: How else do you influence the sport?

A: I'm sure you've heard the athletes' testimonies.

Q: Ex-Packer Reggie White told reporters you helped his team win the Super Bowl in 1997. True?

A: [Nodding wistfully] New England didn't have a prayer. Reggie and I sacked Drew Bledsoe three times that day, setting a new Super Bowl record!

Q: Speaking of Reggie White, he once announced that you told him to retire. Then, two days later, he announced you changed your mind and wanted him to return for a final, triumphant season. But then the Packers were painfully defeated in the wild-card play-offs. Did you forsake him?

A: What can I say? Elway and Davis were having a heck of a year, so halfway through the season I decided to go with the Broncos. But don't weep for Reggie—he made a bundle. I take care of my boys.

Q: So, you're a fickle fan?

A: Show me one who isn't.

Q: Back to Deion Sanders for a minute . . .

A: Prime time! Love the do-rag with "Jesus" written across the front. *Love* the "Holy Ghost dance" in the end zone. Deion's my man!

Q: I once heard him say in an interview, "That wasn't Deion Sanders you saw score that touchdown today. That was Jesus." Any comment?

A: What do you mean?

Q: Does a ninety-yard kickoff return really, as he says, *glorify* you?

A: What if Deion said, "That wasn't me who scored that touchdown. That was John Spalding." Wouldn't you feel glorified?

Q: I don't know what I'd feel . . .

A: Well, you would if you loved the game. Plus, a touchdown sends a good message to the kids.

Q: Which is what?

A: That football rules. [The Giants return to the field.] Woo-hoo! Let's crunch some bones, boys!

The Seven Spiritual Keys
to Becoming a Guru

Tonight, we are going to explore the spiritual and scientific mechanics of the miraculous, spontaneous fulfillment of your desire to become a guru, loved by millions and as rich as an NBA superstar. Moments ago, I was in the hall, deep in my ritual prelecture meditation, tapping the power of infinite potentiality and checking my voice mail, when I was approached by a woman. "Excuse me, Doctor," she said. "But I see that this workshop lasts only seven minutes, whereas you used to charge the same six hundred dollars for an entire weekend retreat. How can you possibly impart all the necessary wisdom in seven minutes?"

Believe it or not, not everyone has read my latest bestsellers, *The Seven Keys to Becoming an Affluent Guru* and *Embracing Infinity: The Seven Keys to Immortality*, available at the back table in hardcover and audiotape, and which I will be signing in roughly . . . six and a half minutes. Of course, those of you who have read my books know that in the subatomic structure of the universe, everything that ever was will always be, and that we are immortal. Thus, a seven-minute workshop is actually an eternity—ample "time" for a seminar, wouldn't you say?

The only things you will not receive that previous students got—in the days before I was confronted with the constraints of a national book tour and the demands of an expanding herbal cosmetics empire—are a couple of vegetarian dinners. But you will be pleased to find in your program coupons for a free colonic and a mud bath at any of my wellness centers.

Okay! The first thing you need to know about becoming a guru is that each of you has the potential to be a guru. It is your spiritual inheritance. In fact, there is a guru within you, right now, and all you need to do is awaken him! So let us begin with a visualization exercise.

Close your eyes. Are they shut? Good. Relax. Commit the greatest act of self-love and devote attention to your true Self, your soul. Become aware of your body, feel the temple of your guru. Focus on your stomach now, a happy place—no gastritis today! Enter your duodenum, or maybe the large intestine; it's up to you, just stay within the alimentary canal. Now, allow this awareness of your abdominal cavity to shift to an awareness of your inner guru. Found him? Good! Now, slide him up past your diaphragm and along your esophagus and into your throat. Allow this awareness of your guru to enter your mouth. Using your tongue, explore the way he floats around your teeth and gums. Now, slowly open your eyes. Very good! You've begun to manifest your guru and are ready to receive the seven keys!

The First Key: Adopt the Seven-Step Formula
Eternal truths can seem amorphous to the human mind, so you must structure your spiritual teachings in an easy-to-

follow format. People need steps, laws, and principles that lead them from where they are to where they want to be, a clear path they must be able to grasp over the course of a lunch break—or else you've lost them. Seven is a good number because it is authoritative and divine—the seven days of creation, the seven seals of Revelation. And what is a guru if not authoritative and divine?

The Second Key: Inspire Others, and Others Will Follow

The universe works through dynamic exchange. When you give to others, others will give back. And so when a guru encourages and inspires, reminding his students of their infinite potential to achieve anything they desire, they will respond with devotion and an abundance of financial gifts.

Let's put it another way: Billions of people are on a quest for spiritual truth, yet there are not billions of gurus to lead them. You do the math.

The Third Key: Attract Celebrity Devotees

I believe Marilyn Manson and Carrot Top are still available.

The Fourth Key: Appear on The Oprah Show

Enough said.

The Fifth Key: Conquer Negativity

Every guru will encounter critics and naysayers along the way, particularly once the guru has purchased a home on St. Bart's. Negativity saps one's creative energy, so allow only unfailingly loving and supportive people to enter your physical and psychic space. Lawsuits and restraining orders are effective means of saying no to negativity.

The Sixth Key: Deny That You Are a Guru

First of all, congratulations! If you've followed me this far, you are officially a guru, free to devote each day to actualizing the previous keys in your life, empowered with the knowledge that your mind has already done so. But remember: Though you are a guru, and everyone will know that you are a guru, it's good guru etiquette never to admit that you are one, particularly not to the media. I, for example, am not a guru. Never have been.

The Seventh Key: Continue to Seek, Learn

A guru must never stop growing, absorbing the wisdom and teachings of other gurus. On that note, will you all please join me now at the book table at the rear of the hall.

Ask Job

Dear Job,

My husband and I are worried sick about our three-year-old, Chad. He won't eat carrots. He'll eat his corn, peas, and tomatoes, even his seaweed salad with fat-free ginger dressing, but he won't touch his carrots! We've taken him to therapy and have even done past-life regressions, with no results. Fortunately, this nutritional deficiency hasn't interfered with his soccer or piano lessons. Why is Chad refusing his beta-carotene? Is God punishing us? Also, is age three too late to start him on the cello if he is to become the next Yo-Yo Ma?

—Dangling in Denver

Dear Dangling,

A great wind suddenly swept across the wilderness, destroying my eldest son's house and killing all ten of my children. The same day, the Lord took from me 7,000 sheep, 3,000 camels, and 500 she-asses. He also slew all my servants. Why are the terrors of the Almighty arrayed against me? Lord, why hast thou made me thy mark? Why did I not die at birth, simply drop from the womb and expire?

If only my anguish could be weighed and all my calamity be placed on the scales! The arrows of the Lord are in me, and my soul drinks their poison! . . . But about little Chad. Why not mash his carrots in wine and honey? And what the hell is a cello?

Dear Job,

I am so into this guy in my algebra class. His name is Frank and he's such a hottie!!! I've had a total thing for him all year, and I think he might be the Dawson to my Joey. There's a Sadie Hawkins dance coming up, and I really want to ask him out. I haven't eaten a thing in three weeks and I've lost twenty-two pounds, which I'm totally psyched about, but I've got this huge zit! I've tried everything, and it won't go away. What should I do? I'd rather die than ask Frank out looking like a pizza face. Please help!

—Freaked in Framingham

Dear Freaked,

Ah, yes, afflictions of the skin. The Lord let Satan cover me from head to toe with loathsome and excruciating sores that bled and oozed pus no matter how long I sat in a pile of ashes sobbing and scraping myself with a shard of pottery. My flesh is clothed with worms and dirt. Oh, that God would grant my desire for him to crush me, to let loose his hand and cut me off! This would be my consolation, and I would even exult in pain unsparing! Try this, Freaked: Cry out again and again for thick darkness to seize the day you drew breath, that it may never again see the early rays of dawn because it failed to shut the doors of the womb on you to hide trouble from your eyes. Beyond that, best of luck with Frank!

Dear Job,

Next month, we're hosting our big annual summer splash, and we're wondering if we can get away with not inviting a certain neighborhood couple with whom we're experiencing, let's say, friction. It all started in May, when my husband, Dickie, learned that this particular husband and wife were telling everyone at the club that we bought a Jeep Cherokee instead of a Range Rover because of a bad investment that has forced us to live on my salary alone! Obviously ghastly lies since we just purchased a fabulous, hundred-acre retreat in Montana. Question: Would tongues wag if we excluded these otherwise well-liked cretins from our party?

—Miffed in Myrtle Beach

Dear Miffed,

Believe me, I know, friends can be as treacherous as a torrent bed, like freshets that pass away and are dark with ice where the snow hides itself. In times of heat such "friends" disappear; they simply dry up and vanish. My own friends see my calamity and are afraid. They torment me with accusations of sin and guilt, and they urge me to repent! They whitewash the truth with lies! I advise you to cancel your party altogether, and beg God to judge you and your husband's souls immediately, to number all your steps, and show you where, if anywhere, your feet have gone astray. This is the only way to end your days of suffering amid the ruins of your former life. And plead for sweet death!

Søren Kierkegaard: The Infomercial

I wanted to have an extraordinary life and panic attacks could not be a part of that. . . . I was given a prescription of Paxil (paroxetine HCl). And, I am very happy to say that I no longer suffer from panic attacks.
—FROM "SUPERMODEL BEVERLY JOHNSON TALKS ABOUT PANIC DISORDER," AN ENDORSEMENT INTERVIEW AT SMITHKLINE BEECHAM'S WEBSITE FOR PAXIL

So, Mr. Kierkegaard, when did you start having problems with anxiety? . . . Mr. Kierkegaard? Mr. Kierkegaard?
Huh? Oh, sorry. I caught a wave of euphoria, and I just had to ride it all the way onto the beach. Ahhhh! You were saying . . .

When did you start having problems with anxiety?
Alas, I was in the deepest sense an unfortunate individual who had from the earliest age been nailed fast to one suffering or another, to the verge of insanity. On top of that, my

father made me dress like a sissy—other lads at school
didn't have skirts to their coats.

How did anxiety affect your social life?

I didn't really get out much, until I started taking Prøkil and
moved from dark and dismal Denmark to Rancho Cuca-
monga, out here in California. That's where I met and married my darling wife, Betty.

Yes. But none of that before Prøkil . . .

No, no. We'd spend entire days, Father and I, pacing back
and forth across the living room pretending we were outdoors,
smelling fresh bread at the bakery and waving to passing car-
riages. As we walked, Father would occasionally stop and
gaze on me with that sorrowful countenance. "Poor child,"
he'd say, "you are going into a quiet despair." He never
explained what that meant, but no matter—I understood.

I see, and . . .

After Father died when I was twenty-five, I learned to imitate
his voice to fill the void in my life. "Poor child," I'd tell
myself, sitting on an imaginary park bench, the eternal night
brooding within me, "you are going into a quiet despair."

But that was before Prøkil souped up my serotonin levels
and cleaned my proverbial clock!

Love life?

Well, back then I broke off my engagement to fair Regine
Olsen, whom I loved more than all the *abelskiver* in Copen-

hagen. I thought I was making a religious decision! Like Abraham, another big-time anxiety sufferer.

How do you explain your behavior back then?

Actually, I believed I'd received a divine command to sacrifice what was dearest to me and to forgo any hope of happiness. I thought I'd been called to dump Regine to pursue the solitary life of a religious scribe. My task? To rattle the status quo, challenge people to examine their most cherished beliefs. I guess what they say is right, misery does love company!

What changes did you notice when you started taking Prøkil?

Decreased appetite and sexual drive, sweating, nausea, constipation, slack-jaw drooling, and an urge to skip work and repot houseplants—the usual stuff.

Well, besides the side effects . . .

Oh, Prøkil completely changed my life! I suddenly felt like I was hooked to a cappuccino machine night and day. I now have five beautiful children and I'm pulling in some serious extra cash, without undo toil, stumping for Prøkil and selling Herbalife on the weekends!

And your writing?

I dropped that, got into life insurance. I wouldn't read a book like *Fear and Trembling* or *The Sickness unto Death* or *The Concept of Anxiety*—would you? Much less write one.

Your life sounds full.

Too full! I also joined the Rotary and I teach Sunday school at Robert Schuller's Crystal Cathedral over in Garden Grove.

What advice do you have for others?

I used to think anxiety was crucial for faith, that it somehow made us aware of ourselves as spiritual beings. You know, clued us in to our standing between the finite and the infinite, the temporal and the eternal. Whatever! But I do know this—Prøkil is chicken soup for this man's soul.

The Celestial City

Now just as the gates were opened to let in the men, I looked in after them; and behold, the City shone like the sun, the streets also were paved with gold, and in them walked many men with crowns on their heads, palms in their hands, and golden harps to sing praises withal. . . . Then I saw that there was a way to Hell, even from the Gates of Heaven, as well as from the City of Destruction. So I awoke, and behold it was a dream.

The Garden of Eden

For years, biblical literalists have debated the location of the Garden of Eden. Some say it was north of the Persian Gulf, where the Euphrates and Tigris rivers meet. Others say it was in the Sinai desert. A California-based researcher claims it was in what's now Turkey, and he says he's got satellite pictures to prove it. Alas, they're all wrong.

The Garden of Eden is actually nestled on a quiet residential street in Lucas, Kansas, a small town about two hundred miles west of Kansas City. And unlike the bountiful paradise described in Genesis, it's made almost entirely of cement—more than 113 tons of it. An amalgam of traditional religious imagery and homespun Americana, this bizarre backyard tourist attraction embodies the quirky personal theology of Samuel Perry Dinsmoor—Union Army nurse in the Civil War, farmer, populist reformer, and feisty old coot.

When he died, in 1932 at age eighty-nine, Dinsmoor instructed that he be mummified like an ancient Egyptian, placed in a glass-topped coffin, and put on permanent display in a mausoleum next to his strawberry beds. Any visitor who paid a dollar would be ushered in to view Dinsmoor resting in peace. "If I see them dropping a dollar in the hands of the flunky," the old man wrote, "and I see the dollar, I will give them a smile."

After seventy years of moldering in an airy coffin, Dinsmoor doesn't have enough of a face left to smile with. Which is a shame, because with the collapse of Enron reminding us all of the limitlessness of corporate greed, Dinsmoor would have plenty to smile about.

Dinsmoor was part of a vanishing native breed, once common on the American plains, who believed that unregulated big business is by definition bad—very bad. Dinsmoor had reason to grouse. He moved to Kansas from Illinois to take up farming in the 1880s, when the federal government, in the name of promoting settlement, had allotted railroad companies enormous amounts of property. The railroads had the pick of the best land and helped themselves to stretches some two hundred miles wide. That left the worst of the land for homesteaders, and many soon starved or left. State laws passed by farm voters and meant to protect local planters and consumers were nullified by the federal government, which also sanctioned the railroads' price fixing that drove farmers out.

Dinsmoor wasn't afraid to express his views on all this. In his backyard, he built a series of sculptures depicting the fallen state of man from Eden to the Gilded Age. The sculptures still dwarf the two-story house at Second Street and Kansas Avenue, where Dinsmoor moved after retiring from farming.

In addition to a serpent, Dinsmoor's Eden displays an octopus, a common populist symbol of the monopolies that controlled turn-of-the-century industry. Its huge stone tentacles are wrapped around the waist of a woman and grab at a soldier's food. Above them is a forty-eight-star stone flag. "Aren't we a fool set of voters?" Dinsmoor wrote. "[The monopolies] are protected by the Star-Spangled Banner. That flag protects capital today better than it does humanity."

Though Dinsmoor thought the public had only itself to blame for allowing the government to serve the interests of big business at great harm to the people, his villains are not in question. A jarring tableau in the Garden of Eden, which Dinsmoor called "Labor Crucified," stands forty feet tall: Atop a concrete "tree" the common man hangs crucified at the hands of a banker, a lawyer, a doctor, and a preacher— the "leaders of all who eat cake by the sweat of the other fellow's face."

I didn't travel to a tiny town on the central Kansas plains expecting a lesson in the evils of unbridled greed. I went to the Garden of Eden to see for myself the bizarre cement creation that some guy spent the last two decades of his life erecting on his half-acre lawn. I flew to Wichita, rented a car, and drove some 160 miles north to Lucas. My first full glimpse as I turned the corner did not disappoint. Poised high in a half dozen cement trees, along the sidewalk in front of Dinsmoor's home, were angels with massive wingspans, a horned devil raising a pitchfork, and a growling dog, his mouth lined with real coyote's teeth. The "all-seeing-eye-of-God" hung from a branch on the "tree of life," which is guarded by an angel with a knee-length beard waving a sword.

I was the sole visitor the morning I arrived. The tour guide, a young woman named Jessica, dispatched her garden lore in quick, uninflected bursts. She answered my questions in one or two sentences, and recommended I consult Dinsmoor's own booklet about the place, "The Cabin Home," available in the gift shop.

Born in Ohio in 1843, Dinsmoor had read the Bible several times by the time he reached his teens and was able to quote the Good Book at length. He claimed to have participated in eighteen battles during the war, including Gettysburg and the surrender of Robert E. Lee. Like others who witnessed the bloody disaster of the Civil War, in which both North and South believed God was on their side, Dinsmoor came home questioning the religious certainties of his upbringing. In response, he turned to free thought and deism, which regards God as a remote figure who endows humanity with reason and the responsibility for events on Earth.

In 1870 he married Frances Barlow Journey, a widow with two children. The couple settled outside Lucas, a small but vibrant farm community. They produced five more children. In 1905, at age sixty-two, Dinsmoor moved to town and set about building his Cabin Home, an eleven-room, two-story house made of narrow limestone slabs, which dovetail at the corners to resemble a log cabin. Dinsmoor also built his own furniture, including a desk with a secret compartment in which he stashed his money—so strong was his distrust of banks. A row of cement beer bottles on the back porch is Dinsmoor's comment on Prohibition: "You can't drink booze any more," he explained in his book. "If you can't drink it, look at it; it will help some."

Dinsmoor was a natural showman. The first in Lucas to have electricity, he wired his sculptures so they could be lighted at night. He ran a tube to a hole in the "all-seeing-eye," so he could shout at passersby from his basement, pretending God was speaking to them. His continual additions to the garden were probably a scheme to keep people coming back.

Dinsmoor tested the locals' patience plenty. The fountain he added to his property tapped the town's water main. Shocked town leaders forced Dinsmoor to cover Adam's and Eve's privates with cement loincloths. When Dinsmoor's first wife died, the town insisted that she be interred in the cemetery, not his mausoleum. Dinsmoor complied, then dug her up, put her in the mausoleum, and covered her coffin with steel and cement so they couldn't move her. She rests there today.

Scandal erupted again with his marriage in 1924, at age eighty-one, to his attractive, twenty-year-old Czechoslovakian housekeeper, who bore him two more children. His son John, born in 1929, was listed by *Ripley's Believe It or Not!* as the youngest living son of a Civil War veteran.

For Dinsmoor, however, the true scandal was unchecked capitalism. The Garden of Eden is, for all its looniness, a coherent critique of modern civilization that draws on easily recognizable themes to explain how we got this way.

In a weird way, economics is at the heart of Dinsmoor's theology. One scene depicts a soldier shooting at an Indian, who is in turn firing at a dog that is chasing a fox that hunts a bird eyeing a worm. The worm is eating a leaf. Here, Dinsmoor is playing off Herbert Spencer's theory of social Darwinism—that the strong are not only entitled to prey on the weak but obligated to, for the benefit of all. Wall Street still espouses that philosophy in a mantra: "Greed is good." In Dinsmoor's telling, the devil attempted to destroy humanity by appealing to Adam and Eve's greed.

Dinsmoor doesn't just dwell on our doom—he offers solutions. In another tableau, the Goddess of Liberty has thrust a spear through the head of yet another octopus, its monopolistic tentacles flailing, unable to grasp anything, while below a man and woman use a crosscut saw marked "Ballot" to cut off the government's support of the trust.

Dinsmoor's populist notions combine self-sufficiency and civic-mindedness, a philosophy the residents of Lucas have come to embrace. "Wild," I said when a local store owner asked what I thought of the garden. "Yeah," he responded, "but that Dinsmoor had a lot of good ideas." The opinion is shared by everyone I spoke with there.

At noon in Lucas, an air-raid siren sounds: It's from the fire department, locals are proud to inform you, telling everyone it's time to close up shop and head home for lunch. Main Street's two blocks include Linda's Café, a Chevrolet dealership, a grocery store, and a liquor store. The small cinema, "the only one for at least fifty miles," a resident told me, was built by the community and is run by volunteers as a nonprofit. At the Lucas Country Inn, where I was the only guest at a place that sees mostly hunters, a sign on the communal refrigerator reads: "Do *Not* Put Pheasants in Icemaker!"

There's no ATM in Lucas. Most transactions are nonetheless cashless, made by check or noted in accounts, even at the gas station on the way out of town. "Lucas is a remarkable town," said John Hachmeister, professor of sculpture at the University of Kansas in Lawrence and part owner of the Garden of Eden. "Most small towns out there are shrinking, dying fast," he said. "Lucas is the only one that keeps plugging, and they've got the same struggling agricultural economy everybody else has. The difference in Lucas is the people. In other towns, people think, What's here for me, what can I take? In Lucas, people think, What can I give? They take care of each other. Their basic operating principle is, Despite our differences, we have to work together to keep this place going. And they do."

Lucas's spirit gives us a vision of what America might have been if folks like Dinsmoor had their way. Enron promised its employees the satisfaction of building a new kind of company—just as the railroads promised a new way of life on the prairie. Dinsmoor presumed that there was nothing truly new, that the capitalist bosses would always look out for themselves and expect the government to look out for them too. By mythologizing the march of greed, he hoped to open people's eyes to the system's unchanging nature.

At the very least, it seems he got through to the citizens of Lucas. A Dinsmoorian spirit is alive in the town's Grassroots Arts Center. Opened in 1995, the arts center occupies three buildings on Main Street that were gutted and restored by volunteers. The museum showcases works by Kansas artists who, like Dinsmoor, the "granddaddy of grassroots artists," were completely self-taught and driven by a personal vision to create. Locals, like the center's director, Rosslyn Schultz, applied for and received grants from, among others, the Kansas Humanities Council, the Kansas Arts Commission, and even the National Endowment for the Arts, which enabled them to hire an architect. "But indispensable to the center from day one," Schultz said, "have been the contributions of Lucas High School alumni."

In the fall of 2002, the center hosted *Yesterday's Tomorrows: Past Visions of the American Future,* a traveling exhibition sponsored by the Smithsonian Institution. "Lucas is the smallest community ever to host a Smithsonian exhibit," Schultz said. "It took a lot of work by more than forty people to bring the exhibit here," she said, "but it just shows what a few people can do if they're willing to commit to something they believe in."

Lucas today would make Dinsmoor proud. "Sure, the town has its share of problems," said Hachmeister. "But it truly has come to embody Dinsmoor's populist vision of what's the best in the American people. And more than that," he added, "Lucas represents what all of us want but so few can find—a good, decent community to live in."

Shalom, Y'all!

On a crisp January morning, when most people were struggling with their New Year's resolutions and debating whether the Patriots would get to the Super Bowl, I was snapping my fingers to the Century Ensemble in an old-fashioned Christmas carol sing-along. The Century Ensemble, an eight-member Christian singing group decked out in matching red sweaters, stood center stage in the large auditorium as they led more than a hundred of us through a series of holiday favorites. If there's anything odd about crooning "I'll Be Home for Christmas" only a week after you've hauled your molting Scotch pine off to the dump, the audience of mostly Midwestern retirees, perhaps happy just to be off the bus, didn't seem to think so. They simply stared ahead blankly as they mouthed, "Please have snow and mistletoe/and presents on the tree. . . ."

This was day one of my Holy Land experience. Or rather, so began my visit to the Holy Land Experience—a religious theme park in Orlando, Florida. Located along Interstate 4 and not far from Universal Studios, the Holy Land Experience is a "living biblical museum" set on fifteen acres that presents, in "elaborate and authentic detail," the history of Israel from 1450 B.C. to A.D. 66. The Christmas concert was a last-minute switch. Because of rain, the park canceled an outdoor "historical presentation" at the Temple of the Great King, a half-scale, white-and-gold replica of King Herod's temple. Instead, the Century Ensemble reprised their Christmas medley. "It was a big hit during the holidays," a female employee, dressed in a biblical-era robe and sandals, assured me.

The idea behind the Holy Land Experience is that when you enter the park's Jerusalem City Gate, you're transported two thousand years back to a "spectacular place, overflowing with religious history, rich culture, and vibrant activity." The male Israelite characters have real beards and greet you with an authentic-sounding "Shalom!" Less friendly, clean-shaven Roman soldiers, dressed in breastplates and helmets, occasionally storm by, seeming pissed off, as I supposed was their wont. Battling with its true Holy Land feel are the little touches. Music that takes its cue from Cecil B. DeMille's *Ten Commandments* is piped into every corner of the park. Mexican poinsettias are generously planted among the aloes and pomegranate, fig, and olive trees dutifully marked as indigenous to the Middle East. On the wall inside Jesus' empty tomb hangs a helpful sign: "He Is Not Here for He Is Risen."

Unlike the real Holy Land, the park is easy on the feet. The Qumran Dead Sea Caves are some twenty cubits from Calvary's Garden Tomb. To get there you cross the Via Dolorosa, or "way of suffering," the path Jesus took to his crucifixion. The Holy Land Experience's version of the Via Dolorosa is not particularly somber. Pilgrims following the faux-camel footprints can stop along the way at a concession stand selling Milk & Honey Ice Cream and Thirsty Camel Coolers.

Another difference about this Holy Land: Everyone who works here is a born-again Christian. The $16 million theme park is a nonprofit evangelical ministry created by an ordained Baptist named Marvin Rosenthal. Born Jewish, Rosenthal converted to Christianity as a teenager, attended Dallas Theological Seminary, and became a minister in 1968. He has made it his personal mission to bring as many of his former co-religionists as he can to Christ, and the theme park is one of his tools. He is the founder of Zion's Hope, Inc., which owns and runs the park, "a Bible-believing faith ministry to the Jewish people and the world God so loves."

Jews have not appreciated Rosenthal's attention. When the Holy Land Experience opened in February 2001, the Jewish Defense League picketed it for several days, claiming the "soul-snatching theme park" was an attempt to convert Jews to Christianity. *The New York Times* quoted Rosenthal as having said his goal is to "share the truth of the word of God to all people, including Jewish people."

Muslims hoping to see the Dome of the Rock should not come to the Holy Land Experience. Nor should Jewish visitors be startled if they enter the Shofar Auditorium for "Inspirational Insights from the Bible" and receive a sermon on messianic prophecies urging listeners to "accept Jesus and repent, for soon the Lord will unleash His wrath on all nonbelievers!" Indeed, the Holy Land Experience represents "the land of the Bible where the eternal Son of God came to dwell and will reign over all the earth when He returns."

But should Jesus return to establish his reign in this biblical land, he'll first have to cough up $22 at the ticket window. There, he'll receive a behavioral policy statement. Presumably even the Lord may be asked to leave the park if, for example, he tries to sneak in pets or food, he wears "any kind of costume" or inappropriate attire, or, according to the "Worship Code," he conducts religious activity "deemed by staff to be causing a disturbance." Which means Jesus had better not overturn the money tables at Methuselah's Mosaics, a gift shop where they're asking $953 for a King David harp. The ten-string instrument comes with a certificate of authenticity assuring buyers the replica was made in 1998 by a company based in Evansville, Indiana.

After the Christmas concert, it's lunch at the park's Oasis Palms Café. A plaque outside reads: "My Soul Thirsts . . . For the Living God. Psalm 42:2." Inside, a Moroccan chandelier hangs below a high dome; water bubbles from a well in the middle of the restaurant. Offered on the menu is a mix of Middle Eastern dishes. I was torn between the Sea of Galilee Fish & Chips, a Goliath Burger, and the Bedouin Beef Wrap. Still, I had an easier time deciding than the elderly couple in line ahead of me. Though each dish was displayed for review before you approached the counter to order, they were stymied by the exotic names. "This one says 'Arabian Chicken Wrap,'" the husband said, picking it up for closer examination. "But do you think it's regular chicken? And what's it wrapped in?" I finally ordered the Jaffa Falafel and a diet Coke.

Then I was off to the Wilderness Tabernacle, a twenty-minute sound-and-light show depicting worship rituals at

the time of Moses. The theater was dark, the stage minimal—a campsite with a large tent that was used as a temple
by the twelve tribes of Israel during their forty years of wan-
dering through the desert. An old guy with a white beard and
dressed in Bedouin garb introduced the show. "Shalom,
y'all!" he said. His comment got no reaction, so he added,
"See, we here are the Southern tribe, so we say, 'Shalom,
y'all.'" This got a few chuckles. What we were about to see,
he explained, explored the Old Testament priestly sacrificial
system. "See if you can figure out the meaning of this
drama."

Fortunately, this was not difficult to do. As a narrator's
voice boomed over the sound system, explaining the five
types of ancient sacrifice, from burnt to reparation offerings,
an actor portraying Aaron, Moses' brother and the chief
priest of Exodus, performed them. The highlight of the pro-
duction was the appearance of a high priest, who entered the
back of the temple, the holiest of holies, on Yom Kippur. In
a scene reminiscent of *Raiders of the Lost Ark,* a column of
carbon-dioxide fog blasted out of the Ark of the Covenant,
lights flashed, and thunder rocked the auditorium.

Spectacular as it was, this ritual on the Day of Atonement,
the narrator warned darkly, "provides only temporary atonement." "Does God have a greater plan?" the high priest
asked. "Is our sacrificial system merely a rehearsal for an
ultimate sacrifice? I believe so." Then a nativity image of
Jesus flashed on the screen.

The priest's question was picked up inside King Herod's
temple, which houses a large-screen "Theater of Life."
There a short film entitled *The Seed of Promise* repeats, like

the tabernacle drama, every thirty minutes. The park literature describes the film, without overstating it, as "emotion-
ally immersing." Each blow of the hammer as Jesus is nailed
to the cross pierces the auditorium, and Roman soldiers bat-
ter down the temple doors as priests attempt an animal sacrifice that, we know by now, is not going to save them. The
rest of the film outlines God's plan for salvation—from the
fall of man through God's demand of a sacrifice from Abraham to God himself providing the ultimate sacrifice, Jesus.
At Jesus' death, the film shows the curtain of the temple
tear from top to bottom, symbolizing that in Jesus the Jewish
faith is now complete—or irrelevant, depending on your
interpretation.

The Jewish community's dislike for the Holy Land Experience is understandable. The park's timeline stops at A.D. 66,
a few years before the Romans destroyed the temple, which
many Christians have long considered God's punishment of
the Jews for not accepting Jesus as the Messiah. Jews tend to
believe that their faith outlived the first century.

In *Travels in Hyperreality*, Umberto Eco writes that the
need for replications—from dioramas and wax museums
to theme parks—is distinctly American. Americans are a
people, he says, "obsessed with realism." For something as
intangible as historical information to seem real to us, we
must reincarnate it to serve as a kind of palpable evidence.
Without such a substitute for reality, without an "absolute
fake" that stands in for the real thing, Eco says, the American imagination falters. If so, then perhaps this is particu-

larly true for believing Christians, and especially biblical literalists, whose religion relies heavily on faith. But would any religious theme park appeal to Jews, whose relationship to their faith and history, not to mention to the Holy Land itself, differs vastly from that of Christians and is, for starters, so much more a matter of birth and inheritance? I seriously doubt it.

Jewish themes abound at the Holy Land Experience, and its gift shops are well stocked with menorahs and Star of David necklaces. Yet all the visitors I met were—no surprise—born-again Christians. And the park was suffused with the glow and easy familiarity evangelical Christians tend to exhibit when they're among their own.

Nowhere was this more apparent than at a talk given at a vast model of ancient Jerusalem in a room adjacent to the Shofar Auditorium. The presentation, given by a preacher dressed like an archaeologist in khakis and an Indiana Jones hat, filled the hall. Using a laser pointer, the preacher indicated a stadium. "That's where people rassled in the nude," he said. "Wudn't too smart of Herod, now was it, building a nudist colony next to the temple?" He went on to explain why it baffles him that Jews can't accept Jesus. "After all," he said, "Jesus fulfilled every single prophecy."

As an example, he cited Malachi 4:2: "But for you who fear my name the sun of righteousness shall rise, with healing in its wings." "Now," the preacher said, "that may not sound like it's talking about Jesus, but it is. Jesus wore a prayer shawl, and the fringe of that shawl was called wings. So when Mark 5 tells us a woman was healed by touching the hem of Jesus' garment, she was actually touching his 'wings.' Prophecy was fulfilled!

"Now," he added, "I defy anyone, Jew or Gentile, to deny that."

No one in the room rose to the challenge.

Who Wants to Live Forever?

I was already pondering eternity one morning—an infected file had fried my hard drive, and I was on hold for a tech-support agent—when the doorbell rang. The phone clamped to my ear, I ran up from my basement office to peek out the living room windows at the front porch. I saw two women, one in her early twenties, the other, her mid-forties, both dressed prim and plain like they were headed for church. Oh God, I thought, as I ducked into the half bath to hide. Jehovah's Witnesses.

I ignored the next doorbell chime, and the one after that. The women were in no rush to leave, and tech support, obviously, was in no rush to help me, so after the fourth ring I went to the door.

"Good morning! I'm Trudy," said the older one, in a slight Southern drawl, as she stuck out a hand. I now noticed she wore red lipstick and had a dainty necklace dangling from the top of her turtleneck. "And I'm Sally," said the other, younger one, who looked away as she spoke. They were both sweet as candied citrus peels.

But coy. "It truly is a pleasure to meet you," said Trudy. "We're Bible teachers."

From there on out, Trudy did all the talking. She mentioned they'd just had a lovely chat about Scripture with one of my neighbors. "The Yale professor," said Trudy. Now, I know my neighbors, and none of them are teachers. Could one be secretly moonlighting in astrophysics for some extra scratch? I pressed for details. Trudy said she couldn't remember the woman's name or which house she lived in. She pointed in the general direction of the three other houses on my dead-end street. "That's not important, John," she said quickly, smiling. "But what is important is a question I'd like to ask you this morning."

"Shoot," I said.

"Since the terrible, terrible tragedy of September eleventh," Trudy said, shaking her head at the painful memory of that day, "has it ever occurred to you, John, that maybe God will bring all the world leaders together and establish everlasting peace on Earth?"

No, I said. That had not occurred to me.

Then Trudy handed me a booklet called "Knowledge That Leads to Everlasting Life." As she described how God plans to restore the earth to the Eden it was before the fall of man, I flipped through the booklet. The copyright page confirmed my suspicion: Watchtower Bible and Tract Society of New York.

"Wouldn't you like to have everlasting life, John?" Trudy asked.

I studied Trudy for a moment. She was a woman who believed in a real heaven where the streets are paved with gold. I desperately wanted to avoid hearing about it. Death, I wanted to tell her, is often sad and tragic—lives are cut short, sometimes through violence or after great suffering. But it isn't always. Was the passing of Queen Elizabeth, the Queen Mum, at the ripe age of 101 a tragedy? And after 101 years, would she, or any of us, really want any more living? And with what in tow? What part of us continues ad infinitum?

On the other hand, it's a pretty universally accepted notion that no one wants to die, and we'll do virtually anything to hold on to life. Ancient Egyptian rulers had themselves mummified and placed in pyramids in the expectation of eternal life. Today, you can shell out $28,000 to have yourself cryogenically frozen and stored until medicine finds a cure for what ails you—and a means to reanimate you.

The clincher for me, however, is always whose company I might have to spend eternity in. As Sartre (and Seinfeld) have noted, "Hell is other people." I smiled at Sally and Trudy. "I'm not sure I want to live forever, Trudy." I held the receiver to my ear and, inching the door closed, thanked her and said I really needed to wait for my call.

Nevertheless, that night after dinner I found myself sitting down with "Knowledge That Leads to Everlasting Life." Chapter 1, "You Can Have a Happy Future!" makes a case for life after death: "There is so much on the earth that delights our senses—delicious food, pleasant birdsong, fragrant flowers, beautiful scenery, delightful companionship! . . . Do you think our Creator wants us to die and lose all of this?"

Well, I thought, why not? Of course, we want to enjoy delicious food and pleasant birdsong forever. But is it reasonable to assume God wants that for us, too? The enjoyment of these pleasures doesn't depend on the continued existence of any individual, any more than the smell of flowers and the beauty of the woods depend on any individual plant or tree. People have relished flowers for thousands of years, and perhaps God relishes the feedback. It's just not the same people, or the same flowers.

Attempts to explain our eternal appreciation always get tangled, anyway. Inevitably, eternal life becomes an exclusive club. The founder of the Jehovah's Witnesses, a Pennsylvania haberdasher named Charles Taze Russell, taught that only 144,000 people—no more, no less—will enjoy the glory of heaven. Russell also taught, at the dawn of the last century, that the end was near—that Jesus had invisibly returned to Earth in 1874 and would establish his kingdom in 1914.

When that failed to happen, Russell and his successors readjusted the date, again and again. As the movement approached 144,000 members, they confronted a greater problem: What is the eternal fate of newcomers to the faith? After all, it's difficult to win converts if your idea of eternal paradise excludes them. Today there are almost 6 million Jehovah's Witnesses worldwide, which would leave roughly 5,856,000 of them out in the cold—or the heat.

In 1935 the leaders of the Watchtower Bible and Tract Society, as Jehovah's Witnesses are officially known, announced a solution. Though only the elect few will reach heaven, said Russell's successors, the "great crowd" can achieve everlasting life here on a future "paradise earth."

The hitch is, the masses have to earn it, by sharing their faith. For people like Trudy and Sally, going door-to-door isn't an option; it's a mandate. If they don't, they may spend eternity in the grave.

In a sense, it seems a bit presumptuous to think any of us should be, or deserve to be, immortalized. Jehovah's Witnesses believe, as do most Christians, mystics, spiritualists, et cetera, that in eternal life we're pretty much the same beings we were in temporal life. We retain in the next world our personal identities, the totality of impressions and experiences, thoughts and feelings, that define us in this world. At the resurrection, Jehovah's Witnesses claim, followers will physically pop from the grave. A colorful illustration in "Knowledge That Leads to Everlasting Life" depicts Lazarus rising from the dead smiling, as his family unties his funeral wraps. "Just as Jesus called Lazarus from the tomb," the caption reads, "so millions will be resurrected." Another illustration shows contemporary families hugging as they're reunited along a winding river lined with beds of tropical flowers.

Should Trudy ever return, I'd love to share with her something I realized while reading her tract. Namely that, to know who we will be in the afterlife, we really need only examine who we, as the products of all we absorb, are today. As the saying goes, we are what we eat. To that extent, most of us are literally full of crap. Americans spend $110 billion a year on fast food, and more than half of us are obese or overweight. We feed our minds the same way we do our bodies. Americans watch on average the equivalent of almost sixty days of television each year. And that's not just insipid shows but also thousands of ads and product placements. It's

fair to say that much of what we offer eternity is advertis-
ing—the corporate images and messages we soak up, however unaware, everywhere we go and in everything we do,
from checking our e-mail to running to the store for milk.

We also slave away at the office roughly 87 days a year,
and in some cities we eat up 30 to 40 days a year stuck in
traffic, where we ingest Howard Stern and Rush Limbaugh.
Most of us spend 121 days a year asleep, our bodies and
minds trying to recover from all the abuse and banality we
endure while awake.

Some people believe that in eternity we're somehow puri-
fied of the junk and clutter of daily life. That's a heartening
notion, but it seems like a loophole. If we are purged of all
this earthly trash, what, if anything, will remain of us that is
still recognizably who we were? In life we're aware that our
existence has an expiration date, yet we eat up our time sitting glued to the boob tube in our underwear. What in eternity could possibly compel us, no longer under death's
deadline, to get off our rumps and evolve?

Of course, many faiths teach that the hereafter will
embrace us just as we are. Presumably, then, we'll be allowed
to enter the pearly gates with the remote in one hand, a
bucket of wings in the other. If that's the case, heaven will be
a hell of a lot more tedious and familiar than some religions
have led us to believe. At least it will be easy to adjust to. I
know it will be for me. I feel as if I've already spent an eternity on the phone waiting for tech support.

The Games Behind the Games

"Where are my volunteers?" David Buckner asked no one in particular, as he tapped his watch. The day before the Olympic torch arrived in Salt Lake City, Buckner, a coordinator for Global Outreach, a ministry that sought to harness "the energy and enthusiasm of the Winter Games" for Jesus, had stacks of boxes to unpack, an office piled with tools, paint cans, and building material to organize, and fifteen thousand misplaced pocket ministry guides to deliver across town. By 10:00 A.M., only one of two groups of volunteers scheduled for the morning shift had arrived. This meant that Buckner would have to give his introductory spiel twice.

When the second group showed up an hour later, Buckner took a head count and realized he had almost twice the volunteers he'd requested. "I'll just have to send more people out on roaming ministry," he said, scratching his chin.

Soon the extra bodies, armed with handouts, were off to share their faith at one of the designated hot spots in Salt Lake City—transportation hubs, Gallivan Plaza, the Medals Plaza, and Temple Square, the Church of Jesus Christ of Latter-day Saints' historic ten-acre headquarters complex—the Mormon Vatican.

The Mormons, wary of world opinion, had vowed not to proselytize during the Games. And unless you strayed into Temple Square, where you were considered fair game, they seemed to stick to their promise. David Buckner, however, is not a Mormon. He is a Southern Baptist. The Southern Baptist Convention sent more than twelve hundred souls, mostly from Kentucky, South Carolina, and Georgia, to evangelize at Olympic venues from Salt Lake City and Provo to Park City, Ogden, and Heber City.

Buckner's outpost was the Main Street Coffee House. Located just a block and a half from Temple Square, it is a warm, high-ceilinged space decorated with international flags and Olympic memorabilia, without a hint of Christianity. My first day in Salt Lake City, five days before the Games, I had tea there without realizing what the place actually was. When I told Buckner this the next day, the Kentucky native and student at Golden Gate Baptist Theological Seminary, north of San Francisco, smiled. "That's exactly the effect we're after.

"My goal is for every person who comes in here to see, hear, or read something that will push a button," Buckner said. "Hopefully, that will spark a conversation leading that person to accept Jesus Christ. And if that doesn't happen, at least a button will have been pushed, and they'll go home with some literature. The trick," he added, "is to bring people in."

Outside the coffee house, street performers sang and danced, painted faces, and twisted balloon animals. Inside, a caricature artist offered free sketches. Upstairs, Christian bands played on a stage visible to passersby, and when the bands weren't playing, a huge television showed the Olympic events occurring downtown and in the hills and towns around Salt Lake. As foot traffic slowed to watch, Buckner's volunteers mingled, creating what Buckner calls "intentional encounters." If visitors wanted to get down to business with Jesus, they could visit the coffee house's private prayer room in the back.

The coffee house was one of only two places in Salt Lake that offered free Internet access during the Olympics. The other was Global Outreach's "command center" across town, which boasted its own vast hospitality lounge, while in the parking lot youth choirs, Christian drama groups, and bands performed. Free coffee and water were available under three white tents.

The command center represented the Baptists' sole miscalculation. City officials anticipated some seventy thousand visitors each day would take buses from Pioneer Park on their way to the Olympic venues, but Pioneer Park turned out to be too far from the action, and the command center served mostly off-duty volunteers escaping the crowds at the coffee house and checking in at Global Outreach's administration offices on the second floor.

Under various names, the Southern Baptists have been "doing Olympic ministry" since Lake Placid in 1980. "We've evolved a lot over the years," said Doran Dennis, coordinator for the command center. "For example, we learned that tracts become trash really quickly. That's why at the Atlanta Games we started distributing guides full of inspiring athletes' stories, fun Olympic facts, maps, and events schedules. People don't throw those away. Then in the back there's a gospel presentation that will lead them to Christ."

Global Outreach's preparation for the 2002 Olympics rivaled many of the athletes'. Buckner, on his fourth Olympics, had been in town six months. Dennis, a Johnsonville, South Carolina, native, had been in Salt Lake since graduating from Francis Marion University the previous May. Global Outreach Director Beth Ann Williams had been laying the groundwork in Salt Lake City for two and a half years.

Global Outreach also had tremendous support in the home congregations. "There's the Prayer Partners program," said Dennis. "We've got thousands of people praying for our needs posted on our website." The Kentucky Southern Baptist Convention sponsored something called 24/17—churches across Kentucky took turns praying twenty-four hours a day for the seventeen days of the Olympics.

Ultimately, it was all about saving the damned. "But," Buckner noted, "we strive to witness in a positive, non-threatening manner. We're not just shoving tracts in people's faces. We're here to meet needs. What I tell volunteers is, if you meet a person's need—whether it's with a balloon animal or a cup of coffee—then you're entitled to share your faith with them." One group of volunteers from Florida arrived at the coffee house jubilant about their spiritual victory on the train ride from the local church where they're staying. "I got to talking with this lady," one woman said, "and I led her to Jesus right there!"

Not everybody agrees that a conversation struck up over a balloon animal warrants a discourse on John 3:16—least of all Mormons, who constitute 63 percent of Utah's population and consider Salt Lake City their turf alone. Though Mormons and Baptists share strong family values and conservative politics, the theological chasm dividing them is unbreachable. Most Southern Baptists consider the Mormon Church a cult. The Mormons, whose founder, Joseph Smith, claimed God revealed all other churches to be false, find Baptists' adherence to the doctrine of the Trinity and their insistence that Scripture is limited to the Old and New Testaments abominable.

But it is missionary work that has stoked tensions between America's two fastest growing major faiths. Mormons are still angered by the Southern Baptist assault on Salt Lake in 1998, when the Baptists chose the city for their annual convention. Roughly 50,000 Southern Baptists descended and made no bones about their desire to convert Mormons. Direct mailings went to nearly 400,000 homes. The Baptists ran 150 television commercials and 500 radio spots, placed newspaper ads, and bought billboard space. Some 2,500 of them went door-to-door. To prepare their flocks, 50,000 churches received copies of a seventy-five-minute video called *The Mormon Puzzle*.

It's reasonable to ask whether David Buckner was inviting trouble by sending Southern Baptists to witness in Temple Square. "I don't *send* them anywhere," he said. "I give them a list of locations and let them choose. If they want to tackle Temple Square, more power to them! They've been advised to know their stuff, as well as the LDS teachings. Hopefully," he added, "they'll have a good conversation with the Mormons, and not an ugly confrontation."

What's certain is that Global Outreach personnel encountered Mormons doing their part. On a visit to Temple Square a week earlier, as I ogled the six towering spires of the Salt Lake Temple that became the symbol of the Winter Games, no fewer than twenty-two missionaries approached me. The missionaries were exclusively women in their early twenties and were in pairs. (As any bar manager knows, female bartenders not only draw business but also provoke fewer confrontations with customers.)

The young women smiled a lot and were perky to a fault. They introduced themselves by their last names ("Hi, I'm Sister Sargent") and asked where I was from. They politely described their faith, and asked if I attended a church and whether I had questions about anything I'd learned from the ubiquitous displays and exhibits explaining Mormon history and beliefs. The most probing question I got was "What do you believe a prophet's message to the world today would be?"

Twice I was offered a free copy of *The Book of Mormon*, which I would have gladly accepted, except they wouldn't give me one. They said I had to provide my home address so a missionary could deliver it to my door. I said I'd buy my own copy.

Back at the coffee house, I asked David Buckner if he thought the Mormons would stick to their word not to share their faith beyond Temple Square during the Olympics. "No," he said. "I've not been approached outside Temple

Square, and I don't expect them to pair up and get all nice and come out in force. But I do expect something, mainly because just last week, at a major LDS celebration, one of their twelve apostles stood up and said, 'The Olympics fulfills Joseph Smith's prophecy that the world will come to our feet, and that kings and queens and nations will seek us out.'"

The Baptists planned to keep the Main Street Coffee House operating after the Olympics closed. A local Southern Baptist church leased the retail space for four years and intended to hold services on the second floor. I asked Buckner how the Mormons would react if they knew there was an evangelical ministry masked as a coffee house just off Temple Square. "I have no idea," he said. "From a PR perspective, they'd probably do nothing. They want to be considered a Christian denomination, so it would look bad if they closed down a Christian coffee shop. But they could really make it hard for us.

"For example," Buckner added, "one of our staff members, who lives next to a ward—a Mormon church—was putting a roof on his house. One of the Mormon men walked over and said, 'Hey, you got a permit for that?' Within an hour or so somebody from whatever department showed up and told them to stop work. That's how they handle Christian organizations.

"As for the coffee shop," he continued, "they had to jump through a lot of hoops to open this in six months. But it was not nearly the ordeal it could have been if the Mormons knew it was Christian." After a pause, he added, "It was an act of God that cleared the path for all this to happen."

Santiago!

"It is not a normal person who walks to Santiago," said the man behind the desk at the Accueil Saint-Jacques, the welcome center for those making the trek of more than five hundred miles across northern Spain to the tomb of St. James, in Santiago de Compostela. The man was short and stocky, about seventy years old, tanned with a gray mustache. He was leafing through a register of names and didn't look up as he spoke. It struck me as an odd greeting. Some of my friends and family, who knew me as a lapsed Protestant, thought it strange I was undertaking an ancient and rugged pilgrimage mostly attempted by Catholics in the way many of my generation took backpacking larks in Montana or Arizona. I'd never backpacked before and had no idea what to expect from the journey. Still, the last place I expected flak was at the pilgrim welcome center.

"Not normal?" I said.

"No," he said, looking up finally. "Not normal, I think." He offered me a seat and introduced himself as Albert— "Albert from Germany." He'd walked to Santiago twice, he said, most recently five years earlier, after retiring as an economist. Now he volunteered at the welcome center in St. Jean Pied-de-Port, a small town at the foot of the French

Pyrenees, a popular starting point for the Camino de Santiago, or Way of St. James, as the old route is called. At the height of its popularity in the Middle Ages, the camino drew a half million pilgrims each year. Today, the pilgrimage annually attracts tens of thousands of—apparently abnormal—seekers.

"I ask you," he said. "Does the normal person spend four to six weeks walking alone viz his thoughts, through the rain and mud, under the hot Spanish sun? No, the normal person goes to the beach to relax!" He laughed. I laughed. But for the first time it struck me that there might be an unsettling truth in his statement. I'd come to escape the routine of daily life. I was drawn by the mental and physical challenge of trudging long distances over a varied terrain that includes five passes above 3,300 feet and offers some of the most breathtaking and unspoiled scenery anywhere. I was lured by the promise of contact with an ancient world I'd encountered mostly through books—more than a thousand years of European religious art, architecture, and history.

But I was an odd candidate for the walk. For centuries, pilgrims have made the arduous journey to Santiago as an expression of devotion to St. James—a voluntary suffering, a sacrifice of pain, that mirrors Christ's pain. Others sought penance for sins or miracle cures for themselves or loved ones. Famous early pilgrims include St. Godric of Norfolk, El Cid, St. Francis of Assisi, John of Gaunt, and Lorenzo de Medici. In the Jubilee Year of 2000, two years after I made the trek, Pope John Paul II granted a plenary indulgence for all who completed—on foot, bicycle, or horseback—the final hundred-mile portion of the camino. My mental and physical preparations were rigorous. I spent six months getting ready for my pilgrimage—reading, running ten miles a day, and studying. I took intensive Spanish courses at the Instituto Cervantes in New York and a graduate seminar in medieval art at CUNY. But none of this settled my mind on the religious or spiritual aspects of the journey.

As dubious as my motives may have been, I took consolation in the fact that much about the camino itself is questionable. Murkiest perhaps is the very shrine of the road's patron saint, the apostle James, whose bones are supposedly entombed in the cathedral at Santiago. One story goes that, after Jesus' death, James went to Spain to convert the western end of the known world, and failed dismally. When he returned to the Holy Land, King Herod had him beheaded. James's two disciples were instructed in a dream to return the apostle's head and corpse to Spain, which they did, in a stone boat guided by the Virgin Mary. Some academics contend that a scribe translating the Acts of the Apostles may have confused the Latin word for Jerusalem, *Hierosolyma*, with the Latin word for Spain, *Hispania*.

For centuries, devotees would later maintain, the body of James lay hidden somewhere in the northwest corner of the Iberian Peninsula. Then, in A.D. 814, a hermit named Pelayo saw a bright star appear in the sky above a hill accompanied by strange, celestial music. He reported his vision to the local bishop, who formed an excavation party that found, directly under the star, a tomb containing the saint, his head miraculously intact, and his two disciples. Word reached Rome, and the pope declared the spot an official pilgrimage site. Soon pilgrims from all over Europe were flocking to the town named Santiago de Compostela—St. James of the Field of the Star.

For the church, the discovery of St. James's remains was a godsend, so to speak. In the ninth century, the Moors had conquered all of Spain except the northern part, through which the camino winds. Not only did the Moorish armies outnumber the Christians but they had Muhammad. Their prophet, whose arm was said to be enshrined in southern Spain, appeared in the sky on horseback, leading the Moors into combat. Christendom desperately needed the relics and patronage of a saint to rally the troops. In James, Spain found not only its war cry—*Santiago!*—but a formidable match for Muhammad. According to another legend, James made his military debut at the Battle of Clavijo in 834, where he slew sixty thousand Moors. Statues in churches across the camino pay tribute to Santiago Matamoros— St. James the Moorslayer—depicting the apostle as a warrior mounted on a charging horse, brandishing a sword, and trampling piles of flailing infidels.

Who knows whose bones really rest in Santiago? In 1884 the Holy See studied the enshrined remains, and five years later Pope Leo XIII issued an apostolic letter asserting they belonged to St. James and his disciples. But there's no evidence, biblical or historical, that James ever went anywhere near Spain.

Albert from Germany spread a map of the camino across the desk. Routes from Paris, Vézelay, and Le Puy pass through St. Jean, while a road from Arles enters Spain through Somport. From St. Jean, the camino crosses the Pyrenees and travels south along the rocky hills of Spanish Basque country. Soon after passing Pamplona the road turns west—a long, jagged line through the wine valleys of La Rioja, across the sun-baked plains of Castile and León, over the lush, green mountains of Galicia, and finally down into the cathedral city of Santiago. "This is not a promenade, my friend," Albert said, running a finger across the map. "This is hard work. Sometimes very hard work!"

He laid out the rules of the road. Pilgrims who produce a valid *credencial,* or pilgrim's passport, may use the free (or extremely cheap) *refugios,* or hostels. (I was ahead of the game: I'd ordered a credencial by mail through the Confraternity of St. James, an organization of camino devotees based in London.) Refugios are simple, coed shelters with bunk beds (bare mattresses on which to toss a sleeping bag), bathrooms, and a kitchen. Many, but not all, have hot water. "You are allowed one night at a refugio, and one night only," Albert pronounced, pounding the desk with Teutonic authority. "Then, you must move—unless you are sick." He urged me to get my credencial stamped and dated at each place I stayed. When I reached Santiago, I could present it at the Office of Pilgrims, near the cathedral, and receive a "Compostela," a medieval pilgrimage certificate of completion.

Against Albert's advice, I got a late start my first day. He said that the hike, which involved crossing the Pyrenees into Spain, would be hard—"a baptism of fire." It wasn't so much the distance, he said, some fifteen miles, but the elevation, which ascends to 4,700 feet above sea level. He suggested I give myself seven hours to reach my destination, Roncesvalles, a small village consisting of a few houses, a restaurant, a bar, and the Augustinian monastery I'd stay at.

"You'd be wise," he cautioned, "to leave viz ze other pilgrims before eight." Eager to explore St. Jean's charming cobbled side streets and medieval fortress, I didn't hit the road till after ten.

The first few hours made for exhilarating, solitary hiking. The sky was clear, the air mild, the views of the valleys below and the rolling hills beyond spectacular. I photographed horses, cows, and flocks of sheep. A beret-topped Basque farmer escorting chickens along the road stopped to let me pass, waving and wishing me a safe trip. But as I climbed higher, dark clouds rolled in, the wind picked up, and the temperature dropped. The mountainside became rocky and barren.

As I neared the summit, it suddenly poured. The wind grew so fierce I couldn't hear my own voice. I dug out of my backpack my light hooded jacket, the one I'd almost left home, wondering if I'd really need one crossing Spain in the summer. Even with the jacket, I was soon soaked to the bone. My teeth chattering from the cold, I barreled on as fast as I could. There wasn't another soul in sight. Occasionally I'd pass a stone marker adorned with flowers and inscribed with a person's name. One name was followed by "Le Puy—Santiago, 1990." As the weather didn't subside, I became increasingly worried by these memorials for pilgrims who hadn't made it.

Shortly after I passed the Spanish border, the rain stopped, the grass route turned to asphalt, and I entered a forest of beech trees. It was here, in a valley on the Spanish side of the Pyrenees, that the army of Charlemagne, the first Holy Roman emperor, fought the Arabs, a story immortalized in the medieval epic the *Chanson de Roland*. On the descent to Roncesvalles, I caught up with a church group from Pamplona out for a scenic stroll. One of the men explained to me that a bus had deposited them a short ways back. I must have looked like a mess, because he gazed at me and laughed. "Why would we walk up a mountain?" he said.

I made good time, reaching the monastery by three. Dozens of tired and dirty pilgrims were milling around outside the dormitory. I hand-washed my clothes and secured an upper bunk in the dorm, a long, open room with fifty beds. That evening I joined my fellow pilgrims for a mass in Spanish at the thirteenth-century Collegiate Church, during which the priest read an eight-hundred-year-old pilgrim's blessing. After dinner at the restaurant (delicious fresh trout served with french fries topped with mayonnaise), I was reluctant to head back to the dorm, which was packed to capacity, so I walked the quiet, landscaped grounds. When I returned at ten, the door was closed, the lights were off, and most people were already in bed.

Predictably, after a brief overture of shifting bodies and whispers in various languages, the room began to shake with a loud chorus of deep, rattling snores. The loudest issued from the heavy Italian in the bunk next to mine. Occasionally, his pattern was broken by a bout of reflux I could actually hear rush into his throat. He'd choke, swallow, roll over, and resume snoring. On top of all this, the monastery bells chimed every fifteen minutes, ringing once at quarter past, twice at half past, and three times at quarter till. That night, I asked myself, What I am doing here? When I had signed in earlier, the monk at the desk asked me to check off my motivation for

undertaking the pilgrimage. The options provided were religious, spiritual, cultural, recreational, and other. I marked
"other," beside which I wrote "all of the above." But as I lay in
bed I began to wonder whether my reasons for doing this pilgrimage were good enough.

In my waking hours, my doubts lessened, and my concerns about my worthiness as a pilgrim faded the more of my
fellow pilgrims I met. It wasn't that they didn't care about the
worthiness issue but *that they cared so much.* Debates raged
in refugio kitchens about who is and who isn't a true pilgrim.
Some maintained that only walkers—and not cyclists—are
authentic. Foot pilgrims, they said, had tradition on their
side, and part of that tradition involved hardship and suffering, which cyclists compromised by sailing all the way to
Santiago on paved and clearly marked roads. Cyclists coun-
tered that they covered the same distance as those on foot
and endured plenty of hardships, from flat tires to trucks on
the highways.

Some insisted that true pilgrims stayed only in refugios,
with other pilgrims, where they belonged. Those who lodged
in hotels were tainted. Most pilgrims I met agreed on one
thing—a pilgrim should never travel any part of the camino
by transportation. A few pilgrims, however, took buses into
and out of cities like Logroño and León. What, they argued,
could possibly be authentic about hiking across urban outer
limits clotted with traffic, commercial sprawl, factories, and
slums? The key didn't seem to be asceticism. From Villadan-
gos del Páramo, just outside León, to the outskirts of Santiago, I traveled with a group of young Spaniards, ferocious
partyers by night, who attended mass every day. They had no

qualms about staying at a local fiesta well beyond a refugio's 10:00 or 11:00 P.M. curfew and jimmying a window if they returned to find the door locked. But as Arturo, their chain-smoking ringleader with Enrique Iglesias looks, explained to me, "If we skip a mass, our journey is pointless."

Some pilgrims stumble upon the reason for their journey as they undertake it. After roughly two weeks, I caught up with a middle-aged German pilgrim named Josef, a physician from a small town near Worms. We walked a segment typical of that part of the camino—long stretches of scrub forests and steep ridges set between tiny stone villages that feel like ghost towns, the nearest city days away. The refugios aren't crowded there, and I hadn't walked with anyone that week, so I welcomed Josef's company. He didn't yet know, he told me, why he was walking to Santiago. His reason, he said, would reveal itself to him as he crossed the Castilian *meseta,* a few days ahead. The meseta is an austere landscape "as flat as your Texas," with nothing to see in any direction but wheat. Beginning just past the city of Burgos, it takes roughly a week to cross. "Under the blazing sun," he said, in a soft, grave voice, "your imagination plays tricks on you, and you see things. Some people have lost their minds there. Gone crazy. My spiritual adviser said that is where God will tell me my motivation."

I never saw Josef again, but I was curious about what he experienced on the plains. I loved the silence and serenity of the meseta, the open spaces and hypnotic waves of wheat. But I was not struck by any revelations.

Gradually, I formed my own rules. I vowed to walk the entire way to Santiago. No buses, cars, or trains. But I caved on staying in hotels—occasionally. I wanted to visit as many historic sites as possible, and in some cities that demanded an extra day's stay. In Burgos, I spent an afternoon exploring the magnificent thirteenth-century Gothic cathedral, the third largest in Spain. It houses the tomb of El Cid and, in the Capilla del Santo Cristo, one of the camino's innumerable must-see curiosities: On an eerily lifelike medieval crucifix, Jesus' flesh is made of buffalo skin and his hair and beard are human; according to legend, they miraculously grow. Once a month someone comes to cut it, said my guide, adding that it's foolish to ask who cuts the statue's hair: If you return a month later you'll find Jesus' hair is the same length. Obviously, someone has snipped it. His matter-of-fact delivery made it difficult to read his take on this bit of medieval logic. He also said that in days of old, Jesus' wounded side bled, a miracle made possible, he admitted, by a mechanism in the Lord's chest from which a dark liquid was squeezed like catsup from a bottle.

León was another city whose attractions convinced me to tarry. In his twelfth-century *Pilgrim's Guide*, the Benedictine monk Aymeric Picaud recommends a stop at León's Real Basilica de San Isidoro—a Romanesque church so named because it holds the relics of San Isidoro, one of the four saints' bodies that pilgrims should visit. The basilica's crypt also has the remarkable ceiling frescoes that have made it the "Sistine Chapel of Spanish Romanesque Art." In a village outside Ponferrada, a night in a plush double that cost less than twenty dollars gave me a day to roam the ruins of an enormous medieval fort built by the Knights Templar. A secretive and much-feared order of mercenaries enlisted by the church during the Crusades, the Templars, legend says, buried the Holy Grail somewhere on the grounds of their castle.

Weeks earlier, however, in Pamplona, I had checked into the Hotel La Perla, overlooking the Plaza del Castillo, to make a pilgrimage of another kind. Ernest Hemingway, of whom there's a statue at the city's bullfight stadium, frequently stayed at La Perla, and I scored his favorite room—number 217.

But staying in hotels often made me glum. It halted the rhythm and continuous forward motion established by the camino. There's comfort and purpose to the cycle of rising early, hitting the road, and stopping for lunch at a village bar (and in most villages the bar is the only place to eat), of arriving at a refugio, claiming a bunk, scrubbing laundry, improvising a potluck dinner, and sharing a bottle of wine and the day's gossip with fellow pilgrims. To disengage from this routine for just a day, however refreshing, means that a wave of familiar faces, friends and foes, will press on the following day without you—and that you may not see them again. To retreat back to the nonpilgrim world, in which people go about their own business, preoccupied with office politics and the six o'clock news, can be disorienting. And as depressing, I imagine, as it is for some of those losers on *Survivor* after they've been voted off the island. Sitting alone in a hotel one night I considered the allure of cults in a way I hadn't since I broke from the evangelical Christian church of my youth.

By and large, I adhered to the camino's rituals and traditions, if sometimes in the same spirit I mumble "Happy Birthday" at parties—not really wanting to sing but not wanting to spoil the fun. Not far past the deserted village of Foncebadón, about three weeks into the camino, there's a pass, more than five thousand feet above sea level, which is crowned by la Cruz de Ferro. It's a small iron cross attached to a twenty-foot-tall oak beam that stands on a massive pile of rocks. According to legend, all passing pilgrims should add a stone, representing a sin or a burden they bear, at the base of the cross. The group of twentysomething Spaniards I was with had, to my surprise, each packed a stone from home and solemnly placed it at the cross. All eyes turned to me. I showed them my rock, which I'd picked up off the ground when no one was looking, and tossed it on the heap.

For two weeks I dutifully wore a large scallop shell, the traditional pilgrim's badge, around my neck. According to legend, St. James's first miracle occurred upon the arrival of his remains at the shores of Galicia. A man who had just drowned suddenly rose from the surf, alive and covered with scallop shells. Pilgrims still proudly display their shells— stringing them into a necklace, as I did, or affixing them to their hats or packs—and consider them sources of luck. I respected the shell's symbolism but found it a nuisance to wear, so I tucked it away in my bag.

Friendships are easily formed on the camino, as the shared joys and trials of the road unite people who might otherwise have nothing in common. For several days I walked with a real-estate agent from the French Riviera, then a young Canadian who professed a hatred toward all Americans. I spent two days on the camino talking theology with a Jesuit priest from Madrid. For almost two weeks I was in and out of the company of a stubborn, seventy-three-year-old Swiss ex-businessman named Werner who spoke little English. He was in terrible shape—he hobbled rather than walked, and puffed red-faced with each step. Yet he was undertaking his third camino in three straight years. He fiercely defended his authenticity as a pilgrim, despite the fact that he rode buses, stayed in hotels, and kept a list of housewives in villages from Pamplona to Santiago whom he paid to wash his clothes. "My wife does my laundry at home," Werner insisted, "and I refuse to do it myself on the camino!"

I found my complete opposite, pilgrimwise, in Erika. A nineteen-year-old German girl who'd just graduated high school—she graduated one day and was on a train to St. Jean the next—Erika did the whole thing on a whim, after a family friend had recommended the camino a month earlier. She didn't wear a watch or have a guidebook. She hiked in sneakers and flip-flops. Her interest in the camino was simple—fresh air. Yet we covered half the province of Navarra together, solely because we were always the last to leave the refugio and we walked at the same brisk clip.

Marco was a thirty-eight-year-old Frenchman and devout Catholic who confessed to me after we were on the road together an hour that he was a sex addict. Marco was convinced he'd conquer his demons by the time he reached Santiago. After that, he would travel to Finisterre, a coastal town fifty miles west of Santiago. There, he said, he would jump naked into the ocean—"and I will come out a new man! It will be a miracle!" Then he'd burn his clothes and return home to settle down with his current girlfriend. (I hope this miracle worked out better for Marco than another he expected with unshakable faith—a universal harmonic convergence in the year 2000.)

This is part of the otherworldliness of the camino, the startling candor of pilgrims who, like strangers at a bar, open up in a way they can't with others in their everyday lives. A Dutch pilgrim in his mid-fifties, whom I talked to over coffee at a restaurant and never saw again, told me, out of the blue, that in the past year he'd been fired in disgrace from his job as a school principal and that within months his parents, four siblings, and closest friend had all died. He described the various illnesses and accidents that had claimed his loved ones and told me, without a trace of emotion, that he had no idea what he was going to do next. Even in some of the most lighthearted encounters, I often knew more about a fellow sojourner after a day's walk than I did about many colleagues I'd worked with for years.

I picked up the pace my last five days. The refugios grew increasingly crowded, often teeming with loud Spanish school groups. Sometimes I'd stagger into a refugio only to find that a busload of kids had just arrived and taken all the bunks. I'd either sleep on the floor or hoist my pack and press on to the next town, in search of a smaller refugio or a hotel. I became edgy and withdrawn. Whereas I used to be amused by the petty pilgrim melodramas that would erupt, like bad reality TV, in the refugios I now had little patience for them. I walked solo, determined to reach my destination, which felt almost tangible. In a two-day burst I covered fifty-five miles, ripping over gentle rustic hills and along damp eucalyptus footpaths, with no thought of pit stops for history and architecture.

Late in the afternoon of my thirty-fifth day, I reached the Monte del Gozo, the Mount of Joy, a summit offering my first glimpse of the Holy City of Santiago, the cathedral's three gray steeples rising above a sea of red-tile roofs. From where I stood, the rest of the journey was an easy six-mile downhill stroll. All I had left to do was enter the cathedral's Portico de la Gloria, join the line to give the statue of the mysterious St. James a hug, and collect my Compostela. Reluctant, perhaps unprepared, to make the final push, I decided to stop and savor one last night on the camino. The refugio at Monte del Gozo is a dreary complex of military-style barracks designed to accommodate eight hundred pilgrims. But it was strangely empty when I arrived. I was given a room, with four bunks, all to myself, a first for me at a pilgrims' lodging. I went to a large bar adjoining the cafeteria. The only other patron was a woman in her fifties, badly sunburned with her blistered and bandaged feet propped up on a chair, sitting alone in the corner, sobbing.

So why did I walk to Santiago? In the end, I'm not sure I know. I can no better explain the purpose of the camino than I can the purpose of life. It's meaning is irreducible. If I wanted religion, I could have joined a church. If I'd been looking for exercise, I would have gone to the gym. If it was self-improvement I was after, I'm sure I could have found an adult ed course. The squabbles back in the refugio about true pilgrimhood struck me the most absurd when I was busy doing what pilgrims do—walking the camino. The very act of undertaking the pilgrimage—in all its hardships and weirdness, its

thrills and unexpected pleasures—may well be the only justification for it there is. And maybe that's plenty.

That night I sat alone with a bottle of red wine on the
grassy edge of the Mount of Joy. The air was crisp, and the
starry heavens glittered above and the city lights flickered
below. I felt like a true pilgrim.

About the Author

John D. Spalding writes *The Sick Soul* humor column for Beliefnet.com. He has written for *Maxim, The Week, The Christian Century,* and *Commonweal,* among other publications. A former magazine editor and book publishing professional, he has a bachelor's degree in philosophy and a master's degree from Harvard Divinity School. He lives in Connecticut.